Together:
Networks & Church Planting

Marcus Bigelow and Bobby Harrington

ISBN:
ISBN-13:978-0-615-46636-1

DEDICATION

With deep gratitude, this book is dedicated to all of our Northern California Evangelistic Association and Stadia colleagues (past and present) and especially to our incredible church planters and their families. Your service to the Lord Jesus inspires us; without you, this book would not have been written.

Together we will ... transform lives and communities.

CONTENTS

PREFACE

We are leaders of a church planting organization called Stadia. Marcus is president and Bobby is director of research, development and missional leadership. We wrote this book with a three-fold purpose: 1) to provide a basic introduction to church planting networks, 2) to convince local churches to plant churches through networks and 3) to provide a practical guide on how to participate in a church planting network. Our primary target audience is local church leaders.

This work is more than a book. It is also a field manual which describes in detail some of the key practices utilized in Church Planting Networks. We interviewed the leaders of (what we believe to be) ten of the most important church planting networks, but please note the limited nature of this work. Many other networks exist in North America - including GlocalNet, Forge, Missio, Mosaic, Emerging Leadership Initiative, Inifinity Alliance, Orchard Group and Redeemer Church Planting Center and others (we describe why we have chosen 10 specific networks in the Introduction). Our description of networks is limited in terms of breadth. Our goal is not to give a comprehensive description of church planting networks, just an introduction. This book is an overview, not a dissertation. We limited the geographical scope of our research to North America, especially the United States. Most of our experience and connections are located in the U.S., but I (Bobby) have worked with church planters in Canada (my home country) for many years, as well. This means that we include Canada in our scope, unless explicitly noted. So when we write about church planting networks, we most directly mean North American church planting networks.

In regard to terminology, please note that we use first person singular and plural pronouns to refer to ourselves throughout. When we use the word "we", we are referring to Marcus Bigelow and Bobby Harrington. If one of us tells a story from our experience or make reference to our context, we designate "I" with either "Marcus" or "Bobby".

We use masculine pronouns to refer to church planters. We know that some church planters are female and that many female spouses of church planters play an integral role in planting, but in our experience, the majority of planters are male. For this reason, we use masculine pronouns throughout, knowing that exceptions exist. Also, some church planting organizations allow only male planters, so making general statements in a way that includes men and women in that role would misrepresent some networks.

We give our thanks to all who helped us write this book. Thank you, Tom Nebel, Gary Rohrmayer, John Worcester, Billy Hornsby, Nick Boring, Neil Cole, Scott Thomas, Pat Masek, Dave Ferguson, Todd Wilson, Artie Davis and Mac Lake, for allowing us to interview you. We are honored that you would share with us. Thanks also to Troy McMahon, Dan Maxton, Terry Martell and Larry Sherman for telling us your personal stories of church planting. A special thanks to Ed Stetzer, who gave us an extensive interview and provided insight on how networks and denominations can work together and learn from one another. And thank you, David Limiero, Roger Gibson, Doug Foltz, Kathy Cawley and others for editing help. And a final thanks to Jen Taylor for helping with the original draft and Chad Harrington who spent countless hours researching and writing for this book.

Marcus Bigelow
Bobby Harrington
Spring 2011

PART ONE:

NETWORKS AND CHURCH PLANTING

INTRODUCTION

All the believers were *together* and had everything in common . ... And the Lord added to their number daily those who were being saved.

—Acts 4:32, 47 (NIV)

Together

This is a book about church planting networks so let's start with a definition. A *network* is a group of individuals connected together, and a *church planting network* is a group of church leaders who are connected with each other for the purpose of planting churches. The title, *Together: Networks and Church Planting*, introduces the conclusion to the biggest struggle church planters have today, which is isolation. Together is the opposite of alone. Networks are the answer to aloneness. We believe that no one should ever plant a church alone, without support, without a network.

When I (Bobby) made the decision to plant a church, my children were old enough to share their input and reflect with us on the decision. My daughter was in her early teens, a period of self-consciousness and fear of embarrassment. "Oh no, Dad," she said. "Don't do it! I can see it now: there is a guy up on a stage, playing a guitar and no one shows up." At the time we laughed. I told her, "Don't worry about that honey." Even though I said these words, I thought to myself, "Yes, that would be a heart-breaking thing and I sure hope I don't have that kind of experience." Because we started an attractional church at that time (and it is still the most common

3

type of church plant), launching with a large crowd was important to us.[1]

There are so many challenges when planting a church. Mac Lake from the Launch Network (we will introduce you to this network soon) described a real church plant, where fears like my daughter's actually came to pass on opening day.[2] The sad part of this story is how the lead planter had to deal with it all by himself.

> When we pulled into the parking lot, I was just shocked because there were just so few cars scattered out across this huge elementary school parking lot. It was a couple of minutes before ten o'clock, and service was getting ready to start. As we walked up to the front entrance of the school, there stood a lonely greeter, who was sort of shy and barely spoke to us as we walked in. Then, as we walked in the building, there was just an eerie silence as we walked down a very long hallway. We took a couple of turns that led us down to the theater—it was a beautiful theater with sloped seating, a beautiful stage, and well lit—a church planter's dream for a facility.
>
> When we walked in this room that seated two hundred and fifty people, there were twenty-two people, and I thought, *"Oh my goodness, this guy is in trouble."* I immediately felt the panic that the church planter must have been feeling and looked around the room expecting to see him in there, shaking hands and greeting people, but I didn't see him anywhere. So I figured he was either in the bathroom throwing up because he was so nervous or he was running out back where his wife was warming up the car for a quick get-away.
>
> So he finally comes out . . . you could hear his voice shaking—he was visibly shaking and nervous—but he was able to make it through his message. After the service ended, he dismissed the people and thanked them for coming. My wife and I just hung around until everybody was gone, because I knew this young guy was going to need somebody to be there to pick him up. So we went over to him, and when I looked him in the eye, I could just tell he was hurting—on what was supposed to be the greatest day of his life and one of the most exciting days of his life—he was ready to give up. Here he had just given birth to a brand new church, and he was ready to quit. I got in the car and looked at my wife and said, *"That should never happen!"*

Mac told us that he believed the lead planter was called by God to plant. That wasn't his problem. He had a great marketing strategy, so that wasn't it either. The problem was he lacked support. He had no network and no support system, and because he lacked those basic elements, he made many strategic and spiritual errors—leadership mistakes, lack of funding, coaching, and guidance.

Although Mac had known the planter for only a month, he warned him before he launched, "Wait." The planter went ahead because the advertising mailers had already gone out. It was a needlessly difficult launch.

When we asked Mac how the plant was doing, he said, "still struggling to this day." This is just one example of what happens far too often – church planters move out on their own without adequate funding, without a network, without coaching, and without adequate personal support. We have an alternative vision of what we think should happen in a typical church plant, so we have written this book to tell you about it.

Over the last twenty-five years we have participated in hundreds of church plants across the continent. We have done church planting without a network and we have done it with networks. There is a great difference. Church planting networks create the best environment for church planting. To repeat our definition, a *network* is a group of individuals connected together, and a *church planting network* is a group of church leaders who are connected with each other for the purpose of planting churches.

While our minds are fixed on networks for church planting, we want to be clear—church planting networks are still somewhat nebulous, illusive, and organic, and thus difficult to quantify and explain with absolute clarity. We continue to learn about them all the time. They reflect our era of change and adaptation. Yet our time is ripe for a new kind of collaboration in the Church because of changes in communication methods.

Albert-Laszlo Barbasi, in his book *Linked*, calls networks the "next scientific revolution."[3] With the advent of the internet and a renaissance of technology, the new possibilities of communication open wide doors of opportunity. At the same time, because of the impersonal aspect of technology, people are hungry for personal support and relationships. Networks are the means for many people to connect by taking advantage of the changes brought by technology, while addressing the aloneness that many experience. This book is an attempt to articulate the present state of networks and to point to some hopeful directions for the future.

Our book has two parts. The first part defines church planting networks and their importance in kingdom work. These chapters will answer the questions, *"What is a church planting network?"* and,

"Why are they important?" In regard to *What?* the essential components of a network are people, leaders, and a unifying idea. In regard to *Why?* networks provide the resources, training, and support necessary to plant well.

The second part of the book includes our Stadia story and explanations of some of our best practices. As a church planting organization, we have made the transition to networks; they are the focus of how we now plant churches. We want to tell the story of how we discovered and embraced networks – and how we create and sustain them. This second part of the book gives our take on the practical question, *"How do networks work?"* offering tangible examples and advice that will be helpful for all kinds of church leaders. We will present our story and practices with openness, but we do this with a hesitancy that it may come across like we have it all figured out. We do not. No one has networks all figured out.

After many hours of interviewing leaders across the country, we have chosen to highlight ten networks in North America. Each one rallies together churches and church leaders to plant new churches. We have chosen these ten particular networks, not because they are the only networks in North America (there are lots more), but because they serve as helpful examples:

1) that can teach us much, and/or
2) that are becoming healthy, well-developed networks which push us to keep learning.

These networks provide an introduction—from new to old, trans-denominational to denominational, and big to small—all of which are devoted to church planting for the kingdom of God. The ten networks are described below. We extend our heart-felt gratitude to the leaders of these networks who have helped shape our thinking and have given their time to see this project come to fruition.

The Networks

While other networks exist in the U.S. and around the world, we focus on these for the purpose of this book because, in our experience, these networks have demonstrated significant signs of health and influence. While the specific mission of each organization is contextually nuanced, they are devoted to the kingdom mission—*to seek and save those who are lost.*

Stadia: Marc Bigelow and Bobby Harrington

Both of us (Marcus and Bobby) are a part of Stadia. Originally called the Northern California Evangelistic Association, Stadia is a national and international church planting group which grew out of a local church planting organization. Approximately 200 churches have been planted by this group since the earliest days going back to the 1980s. In the last decade, alone, Stadia has planted over 130 churches, which average around 200 people in attendance every week. Over 80% percent of all Stadia plants are still active. Stadia's mission is to "bring people and churches together to transform lives and communities through church planting." Stadia hopes to start planting over 100 churches a year soon.

Converge Church Planting: Tom Nebel

Converge Church Planting (the church planting branch of Converge Worldwide, formerly Baptist General Conference) started over 500 new churches in the last twenty years. In the next year, 2012, Converge hopes to plant sixty to seventy churches. From 2010 to 2015 they want to plant at least 351 new congregations, some of which will be multi-site. Converge is distinct from the other networks mentioned here because it is also a denomination. They are committed to church planting in healthy ways in which church planters are cared for by networks. As Tom Nebel, the director of Converge Church Planting, puts it, "Starting new churches through a network greatly reduces the risks inherent to planting."[4] For Converge Worldwide, "There is no greater tool for touching unchurched people with the love of Christ" than church planting.[5]

Church Multiplication Associates (CMA): Neil Cole

CMA sends people on mission Neil Cole, a founder of CMA, told us: "For us it starts with disciples on mission."[6] By sending disciples on mission (even early in their faith), they are set in missional DNA for life. They have planted churches around North America and all over the globe: "From the beginning we had a goal that we would train church planting all over the world . . . because the great commission doesn't stop in Southern California—it goes to the ends of the earth."[7] Having more of an organic mindset and outlook on church planting, CMA does not keep track of how many churches they've planted; instead, they let it grow naturally. However, they are strong believers in training, having taken over 2,200 people through their "Greenhouse" training since 2000. Cole estimates at least two churches start *each day* from this Greenhouse training alone. Perhaps this network is the most decentralized network of the ten we highlight.

NewThing: Dave Ferguson

NewThing's mission is "to be a catalyst for a movement of reproducing churches relentlessly dedicated to helping people find their way back to God." NewThing's mission does not stop with planting churches. They want every church to be a church planting church, and each site, campus and leader is expected to multiply. In one word, NewThing is about *reproduction.* Dave Ferguson, lead pastor of Community Christian Church and a founder of NewThing, says they envision one resident (leader in training) at each of their sites every year as a method for exponential planting.

Acts 29: Scott Thomas

Acts 29 was founded on the principle that the modern churches extend the book of Acts by living beyond its 28 chapters. Scott Thomas, president of Acts 29, says, "The book of Acts and the whole thrust of the early church was planting of churches, starting of new works."[8] Their mission is "to band together Christian, evangelical, missional and reformed churches, who for the sake of Jesus and the gospel, plant churches across the United States and the world."[9]

Association of Related Churches (ARC): Billy Hornsby

ARC has planted hundreds of churches all across America and they want to plant 2000 more by 2025 in America and beyond. Billy Hornsby, president of ARC, describes ARC as a "resource house" for planting life-giving churches. They believe that "starting a new local church is the most effective way to make disciples."[10] With an entire coaching staff, they are strongly investing in their leaders as they go out to plant churches. This is a win-win because Hornsby claims of ARC veteran leaders that, "We're better church planters than we've ever been."[11]

Launch: Mac Lake

Launch is a newer network with the mission "to inspire and equip next generation planters to lead strong." They have a vision to plant 1,000 churches in the next ten years through national and eventually international hubs. These hubs are regions with a two-hour radius which will provide assessment, training, mentoring and continued relationships for church planting. They desire to help churches plant churches by providing the necessary support for local church-plant leaders and congregations.

San Diego Church Planting Alliance: John Worcester

The San Diego Church Planting Alliance seeks to double the number of churches in San Diego by 2025 with 800 more churches. It's not just more churches; they want to fill San Diego with *healthy* churches by accelerating what God is already doing in their city. Their vision includes a national impact, but their emphasis is on what God is doing around them in San Diego. This is the most geographically specific network of the ten we highlight.

Vision360: Nick Boring

Nick Boring analogizes Vision360's role by saying that they are like "the Switzerland of the Kingdom of God." He uses this phrase to describe how they provide a sandbox for multiple denominations, networks and "tribes" from various arenas of the kingdom to play. Much of their vision and methodology comes from Bob Roberts's book *Glocalization: How Followers of Jesus Engage a Flat World*, in which Roberts emphasizes how both the global and local domains of society operate to form a glocal culture. The result is that Vision360 works to be city-centric with a "Glocal" impact.

Exponential: Todd Wilson

Todd Wilson is one of the most connected persons in the church planting world of North America. When the National New Church Convention made the transition from being a network gathering focused on church planting among Christian Churches/Churches of Christ to being a broad network focused upon church planting for all kinds of Christian groups and leaders, there was no person better suited to lead it than Todd. Under his leadership the Exponential Conference has become the focus of networks and church planting in North America. Exponential is not directly planting churches, Exponential comes alongside other existing networks and helps accelerate what God is already doing through them. Exponential assumes the posture, 'you can do it, how can we help?' This posture yields credibility and tears down barriers / obstacles to working together across organizational lines. In reality, Exponential is an alliance of networks.

1

COMMON OBJECTIONS TO CHURCH PLANTING

We hope the title of this book piqued your interest in church planting. Maybe you are a pastor or staff person or lay leader or interested in church planting. If so, great! We have written this book with you in mind and for everyone who is concerned about lost people.

The title of this chapter actually begs a bigger question because the book is about how to best plant churches today. Why don't we plant churches? We have found that church leaders often think that it is not their responsibility. "It is something that national leaders should do," they might think. Or "church planting is for evangelistic associations or para-church organizations or denominational organizations." It is not our responsibility, right? We think there is more to consider.

We think church planting today, as it was in the book of Acts, is still the primary responsibility of local churches and the leaders they send out. It was the church in Antioch, where the Bible teaches us that, "While they were worshiping the Lord and fasting, the Holy Spirit said, 'Set apart for me Barnabas and Saul for the work to which I have called them.' So after they had fasted and prayed, they placed their hands on them and sent them off." (Acts 13: 2-3). Paul and Barnabas were sent out by the local church. We think it still works best when the local church sends out church planters. Before we paint the picture of planting churches like this today, we want to deal with some of the concerns people have about church planting.

Concerns about Church Planting

There are lots of people in Christian circles talking about church planting. You likely have lots of questions. And when you start thinking about it, you may have many concerns. There are five common questions or concerns that we face regularly. Let's get these possible objections out of the way and see if there is merit to our general assertion that "you and your church should be involved in church planting."

First Concern: Church Planting Just Seems Like the Latest Fad
Church planting is a fad for many young leaders. Many of them seem to be giving up on traditional churches and their ways of doing things. Church planting represents the new, but will it last? The deeper questions are "Why is it so popular with younger leaders?" and "Why are they disinterested in traditional churches?" and "Why is it that so many churches have trouble retaining people in their twenties today?"[12] When we see many godly young leaders wanting to start something new, it forces us to ask ourselves about the future and the direction of the church.

Response: Church Planting is a Biblical Response to the Needs of a Changing World
Church planting is not merely the latest fad—it's also a biblical response that transcends current trends. The truth that lost people need new churches has always been true. We personally know hundreds of young leaders who want to plant churches or who are planting churches – and some older leaders, too. The single most dominant reason they want to plant churches is to reach lost people. They seem to be acutely aware of the needs of lost people and they desperately want to reach them.

Most of us do not realize it but there are countless communities full of people who are literally dying without Christ, and they do not have a church or a community that shows them the kingdom of God. Many leaders today, both young and old, have been captured by the present reality of the kingdom of God, and they want to break out and start new churches to reach these people. They deeply feel that if it doesn't happen, much will be lost.

C. Peter Wagner's oft repeated statement sums it up for many of us, "The single most effective evangelistic methodology under heaven is planting new churches."[13] It may be that church planting seems like a new trendy thing, but maybe not. We believe so many leaders have joined in because they have come to the same conclusion: church planting is the best hope for countless numbers of lost people in our country.

Second Concern: We Need to Focus on the Growth of Our Church

Church leaders need to focus on the growth of the churches they lead. The great commission given by Jesus has been entrusted to all of us, especially the leaders of the local church. I (Bobby) understand at a personal level what it is like to have limited means for supporting the growth of local churches. I currently serve a church as a lead pastor and last fall, because of various strains on our finances, I had to lay off two key staff members. These men are my friends, and I love them dearly. In such circumstances it was very tempting to cut back on spending for things such as church planting. But we could not do it. We have responsibility to the local church, but I cannot use that as an excuse to neglect the kingdom of God in the world beyond my home church. We do not have that option.

Larger churches do amazing work in establishing multiple campuses because in doing so they are reaching new people and new communities. Some have even taken the next step in the multi-site movement and have embraced the idea of establishing low cost "missional communities." These are small mini-campuses of the church, with Christians who meet in homes and other places to live out the present reality of the kingdom of God. This kind of ministry makes it easy to rationalize, "We do not need to plant churches, because we are doing our part through the expanding campuses of our church."

Response: We Have Obligations to both Our Local Church and the Lost World Beyond

Growing the local church is important, but we have a responsibility to the lost world beyond our locality, as well. We hope and pray for churches to grow in spirit, service, and size, through multi-site churches and missional communities, but none of these compete with church planting. It is not an either-or question-- it is a both-and understanding. Both growing the local church (and her campuses) and planting churches among unreached people are important functions of each church.

There are too many lost people, too many unreached communities, and too many challenges in North America for one church to think the kingdom of God, as it is expressed in their midst, is enough. The kingdom of God is beyond the scope of any one church, no matter how big. The churches in the Bible did not think that they only had responsibility to expand the reach of the kingdom through their ministries. They sent out resources and leaders to other places, because people they would never meet needed the gospel and kingdom. And they often sent resources from poverty, not from wealth (2 Corinthians 8 & 9). The needs of kingdom growth transcend our local expression of church and what our church can do alone. God intends his kingdom to expand beyond each congregation with resources he has entrusted to them!

Third Concern: We Do Not Have the Money

We are currently living in difficult economic times. Debt is high, unemployment is high, financial insecurity is pandemic. Money is tight, causing many to say, "Our church does not have any money for church planting," and others to say, "Church planting would cost a lot, and in addition to our current budget commitments, we have to remember our obligations to foreign missions and the poor."

The money question is a legitimate one and personal for church leaders because it reflects their values. There are individuals and churches doing their best with limited resources. It is both unwise and unloving for outsiders to make judgments in these circumstances. And we must also remember, no one should give "reluctantly or under compulsion, for God loves a cheerful giver" (2 Corinthians 9:7).

Response: Reaching People in North America May Not Be a Priority

How we use our money reflects the priorities of both individuals and the local church. "Show me your checkbook and your calendar," We've heard it said, "and I will show you the things that you really value." Most of us have at least some money for the things that are important to us. Honesty says that most churches have not made reaching North America a priority. As we will show in the next chapter, North Americans—both in the U.S. and Canada—are rapidly turning away from Christianity and planting churches is the proper response. If you join in that effort, we are convinced that God will provide the funds necessary to accomplish his mission.

While it does take finances and resources, we think it is important not to exaggerate the costs. Planting is not as expensive as some think, especially when everyone pitches in what they can, the amount adds up quickly. This is a book about planting churches "together" with other churches and even small churches make significant contributions when working together. We commonly see churches with attendances of less than one hundred make contributions to church planting. For example, in some networks, if five small churches agreed to collaborate and give ten thousand dollars per year to church planting, they could plant a church every three years. Working together can go a long way.

We must emphasize this point: collaboration is the key to limited finances. We challenge the concept of autonomy and independence when it is used to thwart inter-dependence. The churches in the Bible cooperated and collaborated together and they did more than any one of them could ever do alone. It works that way today in church planting networks. You can join with us even with few financial resources.

Fourth Concern: We Do Not Want to Neglect Foreign Missions

This concern is a vitally important one. It is too easy to neglect foreign missions. Jesus gave the great commission to us and it necessitates foreign missions. This is especially true for North Americans who have so many resources compared to the rest of the world. We are blessed by God so that we can be a blessing to others.

15

If we have to pick between foreign missions and church planting at home, it just seems more honorable to focus on other countries because there are so many Christians and we have so much wealth in North America. We also realize that people in other countries may have never met a Christian or heard the gospel. We remind ourselves that everyone deserves to hear the gospel at least once before we focus on those who have likely heard it many times.

Response: We Need Both Foreign and Domestic Church Planting

We recommend the model Jesus' gave for the expansion of the church in Acts 1:8. He said to the apostles, "you will receive power when the Holy Spirit comes on you; and you will be my witnesses in Jerusalem, and in all Judea and Samaria, and to the ends of the earth." We believe in the balance reflected in these verses. We think it is good to focus where we minister, in our home setting. We also want to focus on the regions closer to us (our Judea and Samaria regions). And then we also reach out to the ends of the earth.

This paradigm means that while reaching to the ends of the earth, we also take care of our responsibilities closer to home. We believe that the church in America is in crisis. In the upcoming chapters we want to expose you to the reality that Christianity is rapidly declining here at home and we have a responsibility to do something about it. People that we love in regions other than our own in North America need new churches. Many people that we are currently pastoring in our churches will move to other regions and we want them to find healthy, vibrant churches. We have responsibilities both at home and abroad.

Fifth Concern: We Do Not Know How to Plant Churches

It often sounds very complicated when people talk about planting a church. Many of us do not know about assessments, church planter training, coaching, and the like. Some ask questions like, "Where to you find church planters?" and wonder, "How do you know that they even know how to plant a church." Local layman and church leaders naturally think that such endeavors need to be left to professionals.

Response –A Network Will Guide You through the Process of Church Planting.

If each church worked independently, then most churches would have a hard time planting churches. But as we will show in this book, lay leaders and pastors alike learn how to do it through the processes utilized in church planting networks. Everyone learns together. And there is an extra benefit--every church leader involved has the opportunity to grow and become a better leader through the shared learning.

Our Challenge to Each Other

At the very heart of church planting is a love for the lost—those who do not know life-giving salvation. The terminology in the Bible for the destiny of the saved is heaven and for those who are lost it is hell—the truth of which is unpopular to believe and even more unpopular to live by and talk about. We believe that Jesus is the only sure way of salvation, and in light of this truth, we have two questions that we ask ourselves and other church leaders on a regular basis. We ask these questions here because they hold people back from reaching the lost—the very heart of church planting. Please consider these questions with us as we seek to describe why planting churches through networks is so important:

Do we really believe millions of people in North America are lost without Christ?

We can easily lose clarity over time. We become accustomed to the nuances of the faith and the different beliefs held by different Christians and different churches. Life itself, in all of its complexity, is sometimes hard to put together. We soon realize that we do not know the answers to all the difficult questions. As we grow older, we also realize that some of the things we used to believe turn out to be naive.

We have de-emphasized the fear of hell. We don't hear much about hell in most churches anymore. We also tend to gravitate from the fear of God to the love of God as a motivation when we grow spiritually. If the fear of God is the beginning of wisdom (Prov. 1:7), and if our fear of hell was part of the good motivation that inspired us to turn to Christ in the beginning (Matt. 7:13-14), we soon grow out of that. Some of this is natural as we mature and become more secure with our own eternal destiny (Rom. 8:39). But it is easy to lose balance. Hell is real and many people are going there (Matt. 7:13-14). You might read that last sentence again.

We want to be tolerant. We live with a strong cultural emphasis on tolerance and inclusiveness. We do not want to be judgmental and we lose clarity about the difference between judgmentalism (Matt. 7:1-3) and making good judgments about spiritual things (Matt. 7:14-24). Our convictions get fuzzy. Many hesitate in their confidence about simple things. Is Jesus really "the way, the truth, and the life" (John 14:6)? Is it true that "no one comes to the father, except through him"? Can we say that there is "no other name under heaven, by which people can be saved" (Acts 4:12)?

We forget that God's Glory is at stake. The best thing for a human being is to become a genuine disciple of Jesus. But more importantly, God is worthy of their devotion. God is good and those who become disciples embrace the purpose for which they were created: to love and enjoy God and to glorify him forever (Rev. 21:1ff). God is worthy of everyone's devotion. We need to help everyone know and glorify him.

Are We Intentionally Giving our Best to Seek and Save the Lost?

Intentionality is the single biggest factor in reaching lost people. In my (Bobby) doctoral program, I had to review surveys of the literature on evangelism throughout history, with a focus on the last two hundred and fifty years in the North American history of evangelism. The intentionality principle was my single biggest learning. If we want to reach lost people, it must constantly be one of our top priorities. Denominations, churches, and individuals that are successful at reaching and discipling lost people, without exception, make reaching lost people one of their top ministry priorities.

Evangelistic fellowships make reaching lost people their top priority. It only makes sense: those movements which have been the most focused upon reaching outsiders are the most successful at it. Charles Kelly set out to determine why the Southern Baptists were the fastest growing Protestant Denomination for over five decades. Kelly tells us what he learned: "Southern Baptists have found evangelism to be the logical foundation of their denominational identity and the single most important driving force in their practice."[14] Stated differently, evangelism was the driving force in Southern Baptist churches when they were reaching more people than any other religious group in the United States. Sadly, the most effective group in making converts in the United States at present is the Mormons – by a long shot. Even though they preach about a different Jesus and, at root, they have a different faith, they are very intentional about reaching people. It is tragic that the Mormons now do better than Bible believing Christians when it comes to reaching people. We cannot miss this important lesson.

Evangelistic leaders make reaching lost people their top priority. Tom Rainer and his research team at the Southern Baptist seminary investigated evangelistic church leaders throughout various churches in North America. He writes, "If there was a single characteristic that separated the pastors of effective [evangelistic] churches from other pastors, it was the issue of accountability in personal evangelism."[15] A whopping 43% of pastors established some type of accountability for their own personal evangelism in evangelistic churches, compared to 2% in non-evangelistic churches.

Summary

Now you understand why we want you to join us in reaching lost people and why we want to persuade you about the value of church planting in this quest. You can make a difference. You and your decisions are God's plan. It may be that God has you reading this book for this exact reason. Maybe your efforts at reaching lost people through church planting will make all the difference in the world. Let us state it bluntly, but with optimism – we believe there are people out there who will be rescued from hell, brought into the kingdom, and forever give God glory because of the efforts and decisions that you will make.

We love many things that were spoken or written by Charles Spurgeon. We end this chapter with one of the best exhortations he ever made. It expresses our beliefs succinctly:

> If sinners be damned, at least let them leap to Hell over our dead bodies. And if they perish, let them perish with our arms wrapped about their knees, imploring them to stay. If Hell must be filled, let it be filled in the teeth of our exertions, and let not one go unwarned and unprayed for.[16]

****

We will now unpack the first part of the book (the two parts are described in the introduction), starting with an in-depth theological and practical foundation for church planting in North America. We will then focus on the nature of networks, the leadership dynamics and the principles involved. You will learn that networks often have a national (macro) presence and a local (micro) presence as they function as relational hubs throughout the country. You will see that networks are led on a macro-level by apostolic leaders and on a local micro-level by both apostolic leaders and network coaches. As they catalyze church planting efforts, they transmit unique ideological DNA throughout their network.

We will explore structure, leadership, and ideology. Then by way of a connection with the larger church world, we have one chapter dedicated to the question of how denominations can participate with or function as church planting networks. We conclude the first half of the book by making the case that networks provide the best environment for church planting today by describing the benefits of this type of collaboration.

2

NETWORKS AND THE KINGDOM

In this chapter:
- How church planting aligns with Jesus' desire to seek and save the lost
- The state of the church in North America
- Five core reasons to plant churches

We both planted churches in the 1990s and know the highs and lows, intimately. I (Marcus) planted a church in the early 1980s and then moved on to lead a regional church planting organization, and then to a national leadership role as president when Stadia formed in 2003. Bobby planted in the late 1990s and continues as lead pastor of the church to this day (Harpeth Community Church, by the Harpeth River, just south of Nashville). In 2003 Bobby also joined Stadia. He has served in all kinds of leadership roles, from training church planters and coaches, to helping pioneer Stadia's church planting network system and to his current role in research and development focused on missional church plants. I (Marcus) continue everyday with a singular focus on church planting and church planting networks. For both of us church planting is a dominant theme in everything we do. We are completely sold out to it! This chapter tells you why we have so much passion.

God has a kingdom. We believe he wants everyone saved and added to his kingdom. We believe that church planting is the most effective means of expanding that kingdom—and networks are the most effective way to support church planting. It is that simple: we believe church planting through church planting networks activates God's mission to redeem humanity and restore creation more effectively than any other enterprise.

The Bible does not contain organizational mission and vision statements for the church, but it does teach us what is important. After Jesus stayed at Zacchaeus's home, he said, "Today salvation has come to this house because this man, too, is a son of Abraham. *For the Son of Man came to seek and to save what was lost*" (Luke 19:10). The disciples did not write this statement on a poster, billboard or campaign banner, but it represented Jesus' purpose for humanity—to seek and save the lost. He didn't come just to save their souls but also to make disciples, redeeming their entire lives. He was sent for the coming of the kingdom of God: "I must preach the good news of the kingdom of God to the other towns also, because that is why I was sent" (Luke 4:43). God sent Jesus into the world and God moves the church into the world for the same reason—his kingdom come. Nothing was more prominent in the teaching of Jesus.

At the end of his ministry on earth, Matthew, Mark, and Luke record Jesus' last message to his Apostles—I am sending you to go into the nations. In Matthew he says, "Go and make disciples" (28:19). Mark records, "Go into all the world and preach the good news to all creation" (16:15). Luke writes, "Repentance and forgiveness of sins will be preached in [my] name to all nations, beginning at Jerusalem. You are witnesses of these things." (24:47). His message and ministry were the gospel of the kingdom and he sent his apostles to take that message to the world.

We have heard these passages before—whether in a sermon, a book, or a lecture—but what do they have to do with North America in the twenty-first century? Many of us hear, read and understand the great commission in its various forms with international ears, without giving much credence to North America. Perhaps the reason is because we still believe the U.S. and Canada are Christian nations. Before answering the question, *Why join church planting networks?* we want to survey the landscape of American spirituality and answer the question, *Why church planting in North America?*

The Case for Planting Churches in North America

More believers are awakening to the reality of American spirituality since Gregory Boyd's book, *The Myth of a Christian Nation,* was released and more recently since *Unchristian* by David Kinnaman and Gabe Lyons was published.[17] While the skies of many cities are pinned with steeples, more church doors are closing every year —by the thousands. It's not just the number of churches that is declining--the number of believers is declining as well. As Dave Olson demonstrated in his ground-breaking book, *The American Church in Crisis,* an estimated *82 percent of Americans today do not attend church on any given Sunday* which is also why Josh McDowell described young Christians today as *The Last Christian Generation.*[18]

Although it is hard to peg comparable statistical studies like Olson's and McDowell's in Canada, most Canadian church leaders will say that their decline is even worse than what is happening in the States. One of Canada's foremost experts on the sociology of religion, Reginald Bibby, has demonstrated that while Canadians may not be turning away from belief in "a god or gods," they are turning away from church at a fast rate.[19] If current trends hold, North Americans are following Europe in turning away from church and orthodox Christianity. This situation is tragic. God's heart for the nations beats just as strongly today as it did two thousand years ago. His kingdom is just as powerful now as it was back then.

Why plant churches in America? Because North Americans need Jesus and they need local churches that transform lives and communities in His name! What follows is a five-fold argument for church planting in North America. We do not make this case lightly—it flows through our veins every day, and it is at the very heart of God. North American Christians must plant churches because of the biblical mandate, religious trends, the missional-incarnation impulse, church revitalization and sociological realities.

1. The Biblical Mandate: *The Bible Teaches Us to Start New Churches*

The kingdom mission of Jesus inspired the apostle Paul and others to proclaim the gospel, reach lost people and plant churches. The events that took place required more than human efforts of whim or wit, wisdom and strength; they required the hand of God. The word of God spread and manifested itself in the planting of churches throughout the inhabited Greco-Roman world.

The book of Acts begins and ends with the kingdom of God. Jesus spoke about it for the forty days of his post-resurrection ministry in chapter one: "After his suffering, he showed himself to these men and gave many convincing proofs that he was alive. He appeared to them over a period of forty days and spoke about the *kingdom of God*" (v. 3).

After the expansion of the church throughout the inhabited world, Paul spent all of his time telling people about the gospel of Jesus Christ, focusing on the kingdom in chapter twenty-eight: "They arranged to meet Paul on a certain day, and came in even larger numbers to the place where he was staying. From morning till evening *he explained and declared to them the kingdom of God* and tried to convince them about Jesus from the Law of Moses and from the Prophets" (v. 23; cf. 28:31).

The kingdom bookends Luke's narrative in Acts, but the infiltration of the kingdom into the world characterizes the story as a whole. Where the message was preached, churches emerged. Starting in Jerusalem, the church spread and local congregations formed in Judea and Samaria, Damascus, Antioch, Lystra, Derbe, Iconium, Colossae, Laodicea and to the ends of the earth.

The Apostles did not simply preach a message, they planted churches, too. God's method of kingdom-expansion focuses on His community, the church. The church is the only divinely authorized institution given the task of reaching the world and making disciples. When his people plant churches, God transforms lives and communities. The apostles replicated this mission by planting churches everywhere they went. Most of Paul's letters in the New Testament are addressed to the geographically located churches he planted. The book of Acts describes how the Apostles lived out Jesus' great commission, and they lived it out by planting churches. If *they* planted churches to fulfill his mission, we should too. The mission has not ended—North America increasingly needs new churches.

2. Cultural Trends: *We Desperately Need New Churches*

More and more people in North America live with neither active involvement in church nor biblical discipleship. As we mentioned above, David T. Olson takes a look at the status of the American church in his book *The American Church in Crisis*. His conclusions are grim, but they provide cultural inspiration for the mandate to plant churches. Olson believes that at the rate the American church is declining; by the year 2020, only 14.7 percent of the American population will attend church each weekend.[20] He lists ten changes necessary for the American church to have a bright future. He states, "Established churches must embrace church planting as the primary method of passing the faith on to future generations."[21]

To understand Olson's conclusions, we must take a deeper look at his research. Most studies of religious participation focus on the attitudes people express in opinion surveys. For example, the Barna Research Group and Gallup pollsters conducted surveys recently about church attendance—Barna found that 47 percent of the Americans surveyed said attended church weekly and Gallup found it to be closer to 44 percent.[22] Note that these two studies based their surveys on what people *said* about their attendance. The American Church Research Project, however, claims a much lower percentage of people actually attended church during that year. In 2005, only 17.5 percent of Americans attended an "orthodox Christian church on any given weekend" (including evangelical, mainline and catholic churches).[23] Why such a discrepancy? It is caused by the *halo effect*. It doesn't just affect religious polls—sociologists say it affects polls having to do with politics as well.

The halo effect is an ironic way of describing how people make themselves appear better than they are when being interviewed and it skews statistics. Not everyone tells the truth.
Olson cites the US election of 1996 as a good example of the halo effect. After election polls showed that 58 percent of the adult population *said* they voted.[24] In reality, however, only 49 percent *actually* voted. So Barna's statistic that 47 percent of Americans

attended church weekly was probably not entirely true. Through more qualitative research and analysis, including follow up and visiting churches, 33 percent of Americans go to church semi-regularly (at least once a month), and those who go to church every week is 17.5 percent of the population, which is about half as many who go on a semi-regular basis.[25] We recognize that statistics are not the tell-all sign of spiritual vitality, but they do reveal a significant aspect of the American spiritual climate.

It's not simply that church attendance is going down--the population is also rising. From 1990 to 1996 the American population grew by 51.8 million people.[26] In the same year they completed that study, 51.7 million Americans attended church on any given Sunday according to Olson. Thirty seven hundred churches close their doors each year and 4,000 start every year.[27] The net gain of churches is only 300 churches per year across the nation.

The North American Mission Board looked at the church and population statistics from 1900 and from 2000, concluding that "the number of churches increased just over 50 percent while the population of the country quadrupled."[28] With a steady increase in population size and not enough new churches, the American church will continue declining. In order to simply maintain the percentage of believers, Olson estimates that thousands more churches need to be planted. God's heart is even bigger than that: Paul says that God "wants all men to be saved and to come to a knowledge of the truth," not merely a good percentage of people (1 Tim 2:4). David Olson is right—the American church is in crisis and he's not the only one saying it.

Ed Stetzer, a leading North American missiologist, agrees. He comments on the status of churches: "The spiritual deadness of North America appears not only in its culture but in its churches, as well. Churches in the first decade of the twenty-first century are closing at a phenomenal rate. Eighty to 85 percent of American churches are on the downside of their life cycle."[29] George Hunter goes as far as saying, "the U.S. is the largest mission field in the Western hemisphere," and the "the fifth largest mission field on earth."[30]

As the population in America grows, the church faces a challenge—more people means more redemptive potential, at least numerically. Will the church meet the challenge of an increasing population in the twenty-first century? If she will, we cannot be satisfied with status quo in church growth, size or depth. It's not simply a biblical mandate and cultural trends that necessitate planting churches, the missional nature of the kingdom methods leads us to new peoples—some of whom will not be reached by established churches.

3. The Missional-Incarnational Impulse: *Some communities will not be reached without new churches*

Jesus fulfilled his mission and rescued lost people by entering into their world. He was "missional" (seeking to reach people) and "incarnational" (the embodiment of God's truth). As Alan Hirsh points out, an increasing number of people will not be attracted to traditional churches. [31] Instead, we must take the church into communities to people who are far from God. These are missional-incarnational churches.

In the Nashville, Tennessee area, where I (Bobby) live, many people live far away from grocery stores with healthy food, making it difficult to buy quality food. In certain areas 70 percent of the people must take public transportation to get to a grocery store, but that takes an average of two hours round-trip.[32] Consequently geographical proximity to grocery stores largely determines how many of those people eat healthy food (as opposed to corner stores with unhealthy food). One Vanderbilt medical student decided to create "Nashville Mobile Markets" which are vehicles and trailers going around with healthy food to those who live geographically distant from grocery stores.

When Christian leaders move into a community to demonstrate the truth of Jesus to people who will not or cannot travel to find it, they are doing something similar. How much more important is it for the church to go into dead and lifeless places to plant healthy churches who can give them not only a loaf of fresh bread but the bread of life? It is one thing to invite someone to church, but if we are going to be the missional-incarnational community Jesus demonstrated in the gospels and the church

27

displayed in Acts, we are going to have to intentionally go to the unreached places to seek and save what was lost.

Alan Hirsch points out that the dominant model of church today--called the "attractional church"--likely appeals to about 40 percent of the current population in North America.[33] The other 60 percent of the population (and growing) will require a different approach. More church leaders are finding that they must be missionaries, moving into communities and bring the gospel and the church to the people who live there like Jesus did. Even though the following chart is an over-statement in part, the traditional "attractional church" is contrasted with the "missional-incarnational church".

Attractional Church	Missional Church
Come and *See*	*Go* and *Be* (like Jesus)
Pastors are gifted to serve us	The church is gifted for service
Come to building, programs, staff	*Go love*, serve in the community
Worship at *the church*	Worship by *your life in the community*
Proclamation through the church	Good news/deeds proclaimed
Join us for religious services	Go to the people, serve their needs

Certain groups of people will only be reached by missional-incarnational churches. These types of churches focus on a community life where "the way of Jesus" informs and radically transforms the people in a community because a church was planted to reach the people in that community. Millions of North Americans desperately need a missional-incarnational church in their community. They will only experience one when it is planted among them.

4. Church Revitalization: *Established Churches Need New Churches*

Why don't we invest our efforts in already established churches that are declining? some object.[34] *Should we not try to revive the dying churches that are closing their doors by the thousands?* Tim Keller, the planter of Redeemer Presbyterian Church in New York City, answers this common objection in his convincing article "Why Plant Churches".[35] He says that new churches do not take away from revitalization; instead, planting new churches brings new ideas, leaders, challenges and believers to the body of Christ. These new churches become a platform for discovering innovative methods for reaching their surrounding culture with the gospel of Jesus. New ideas disseminate from these new assemblies into established churches. When the older churches see the movement of God in a new way through a new church, it often causes them to reevaluate their own congregations, causing self-examination and a renewed mindset. When the new church baptizes new believers, some will leave the new church for a more traditional, established church because the new body does not provide the kind of stability they desire.

Finally, many young leaders struggle to relate to the churches that currently exist so they won't step up to lead in a traditional church. If they are given the opportunity, however, to participate in something new, they are often more likely to step up to lead. The truth is that *leaders come from and pour back into the church through church planting whereas they might otherwise have stayed on the sideline.* These leaders, according to Keller, eventually build up the whole city-body.[36]

We believe the church rises and falls on leadership, first on the leadership of the Holy Spirit and second, on the leaders of God's people. We need more leaders and church planting allows a unique avenue through which leaders can emerge to utilize their gifts. For all of these reasons new churches not only expand the kingdom but they also revitalize and resource already established churches, as well.

Similarly, some will say, *Why do we need more churches? Let's just make bigger ones.*[37] The truth is that the age of a church matters more than its size; younger churches evangelize the lost more than older churches evangelize.[38] Aubrey Malphurs notes that "churches under three years of age win an average of ten people to Christ per year for every hundred church members," whereas, "churches over fifteen years of age win an average of three people per year for every hundred church members."[39] Following these statistics, a fifteen-year-old church of 1,000 people baptizes thirty people for Christ per year. But take those same 1,000 people and put them in ten new churches and they will win 100 people to Christ, according to this study. So instead of just thirty new believers, it will be a hundred. New churches are just simply more effective at reaching lost people than established or more traditional churches. This is why so many resonate with C. Peter Wagner's statement referred to in an earlier chapter, when he said, after years of research, "the single most effective evangelistic methodology under heaven is planting new churches."[40] David Jackson, a church planting leader, adds:

> I would go so far as to say that [Wagner's quote] is the most referenced statement about the value of church planting in the last twenty years, though I have nothing but anecdotal evidence to support it. What I can support is that his categorical statement has been researched multiple times since then and it has in every instance of which I am aware (*Christianity Today*, Fuller Seminary doctoral dissertation and LifeWay over the decade from 1991-2001) found him not only to be correct in his assessment, but rather overwhelmingly correct. By a ratio of no less than 3:1, church plants are more effective evangelistically than churches over fifteen (sometimes ten) years of age! Such a researched FACT should rightly be shouted from the mountaintops and proclaimed in every classroom.[41]

Not only do new churches revitalize older churches, but new churches are more effective at reaching lost people than more traditional churches. So church planting does not take away from church revitalization or church growth—church planting catalyzes them.

5. Sociological Realities: *New Generations, People Groups, and Residents Need New Churches*

Jesus taught us that new wine needs new wineskins (Matthew 9:17). If a person tried to put new wine in old wineskins, then the skins would burst. In a like manner, it takes new approaches and structures to support bridging the gospel into new contexts. New generations, people groups, and residents often think very differently about life than those who went before them. The gospel and the kingdom are always new and fresh, but as missionaries, we must show how they apply in these new contexts. New churches are like new wineskins - they are more flexible, adaptable, and resilient in the face of new perspectives, needs and desires.

Keller makes a similar sociological argument for church planting:

- New generations, new people groups and new residents are best reached through church plants.[42]
- New generations are more likely to join a new church because they do not prefer the leadership style, sermon topics and general style of long-established churches.
- New residents who want to be involved in church leadership readily come into the newer rather than the older body because "it may require tenure of 10 years before you are allowed into places of leadership and influence."[43]

New people groups are reached more effectively through new movements of the church because the DNA of established churches is less flexible and more exclusionary by nature of how long it has been functioning. Newer churches more readily embrace new socio-cultural groups (e.g., Hispanics). He summarizes the concept:

> New congregations *empower* new people and new peoples much more quickly and readily than can older churches. Thus they always have and always will reach them with greater facility than long-established churches. This means, of course, that church planting is not only for 'frontier-regions' or 'pagan' countries that we are trying to see *become* Christian. Christian countries will have to maintain vigorous, extensive church planting to simply *stay* Christian.[44]

Church planting always has been and always will be the grid upon which the gospel spreads. The word is sown and people gather together. The very nature of the church, at least in the New Testament, is a gathering of believers.

Summary

Jesus said the kingdom of God is like a mustard seed that starts small and grows large (Mark 4:31). If we are kingdom-minded, we have to be active in the preparing of leaders, sending out planters and planting churches. Church planting and North America belong together because of biblical example, cultural need, missional-incarnational impulse, church renewal and sociological understanding. Because of these truths, we are passionate about how God uses church planting to transform lives and communities.

As we describe church planting networks in this book, we want to be clear that networks are not about expanding a specific model of church--they are about expanding the kingdom of God by planting churches of all kinds. It is upon this kingdom-mission that every church-planting network is founded. Each network articulates its particular organizational mission differently, but one characteristic defines each church-planting network we have studied—a passionate devotion to expanding the kingdom of God through establishing new churches.

3

NETWORKS AND RELATIONSHIPS

In this chapter:
- The need for relational support in church planting
- The general contrasts between denominations and networks
- An introduction to some unique accents in some of the highlighted networks
- A presentation of networks on a national scale (macro) and local scale (micro)

Church planting networks connect people together for the purpose of supporting both healthy leaders and healthy church plants. Ministry is a difficult and often lonely battle, and church planting can feel like the front lines of a war. Scott Thomas recounts an Acts 29 network retreat in Summer 2010 when one man stood up to share his story of desperation:

> This past summer . . . we had the guys share at our retreat. We said, "Would you share how the network has provided some kind of shepherding?" We had a man whose wife was institutionalized after 15 years of marriage tell about how the network really started to fight for him and his marriage. So, while his wife was in the hospital, they paid for a housekeeper to come in and clean the house. Other planters covered his pulpit. They did some counseling, not *to* him, but *for* him. They really ministered to him,

prayed with him and for him. Guys flew up with him to his area and stayed with him during the most critical times. Until they discovered that the problem was a chemical imbalance that was causing her problems, and corrected it.

He shared how he would have killed himself. He literally took off one day in his truck, looking for the best place to kill himself. He said he couldn't take it anymore: "While I was driving, looking for a place to kill myself in my truck," he said, "I kept thinking about all the Acts 29 pastors who had prayed with me, who had called me, who had connected with me, and were standing beside me." Then he closed it by saying, "I could live with killing myself if it was just me, but I don't want to face these brothers." It was powerful. Tears! You never saw so many Acts 29 guys cry in all your life.

Story after story like that surfaced in our gatherings, for example a couple whose baby was born with a defect, and died after two months. There was no life insurance. The Acts 29 guys paid for the funeral, and were there for him, loved on him, and then he announced that they are pregnant again. There are many stories like that. The guys really get it.[45]

These stories are the stories of network relationships. The relationships provided the opportunity for restoration, healing and support for a church planter when he needed it most. Situations like these (and many others) often end differently. It's not always as dramatic as death. Sometimes church planters just get burned out. Some give up because it was harder than they realized. We believe Bob Roberts had it right when he described what should happen in church planting circles. He says, "No one will do anything alone anymore. It will take many people and networks from many places to accomplish business and everything else. The day of the Lone Ranger has passed."[46]

The answer to Bob Robert's challenge is church planting networks. They provide the needed safety net of support. Relational connections characterize church planting networks more than any other element.

Seth Godin, a popular business blogger, has written extensively on networks (except that he calls them *tribes*) and claims they are everywhere, the very fabric of society. In his book, *Tribes,* he defines the term *tribe* broadly: "a group of people connected to one another, connected to a leader, and connected to an idea."[47] Notice the emphasis on "connection." Each person is connected to each other, each leader is connected to the group, and each member is connected to a common idea. These connections are the very essence of a tribe. Without them, there is no network. It's not just a trendy new topic that publishes books. It's rooted in history and in the Word of God.

The strength of the church has always been the connection between people--their relationships. It started with Jesus and his disciples who spent years together. He listened to them, taught them and coached them. He knew them. Jesus was sharing the relationship he had with God, the Father. In the gospel of John, Jesus, the Word, was with God and was God in the beginning (1:1-2). It was this same relationship that Jesus prayed would characterize the church after he finished his ministry on earth.

In the garden of Gethsemane, during his high priestly prayer, he asked God for unity: "I pray also for those who will believe in me through [the Apostles'] message, that all of them may be one, Father, just as you are in me and I am in you. May they also be in us so that the world may believe that you have sent me." One of Jesus' last requests was for a unifying relationship between believers. He finished by praying, "May they be brought to *complete unity to let the world know that you sent me and have loved them even as you have loved me* (John 17:20-21, 23).

Christian connectedness is deeper than any other tribe or group because it comes from God. Any church-planting strategy that leaves out cohesion with God and unity with others is not a Christian church-planting strategy. The very nature of the church—even the Greek word for *church*—is gathering together (e.g., Acts 19:32).

Paul pleads with the church to be unified: "If you have any encouragement from being united with Christ . . . then make my joy complete by being like-minded, having the same love, being one in spirit and purpose" (Philippians 2:1-2). The fruit of the spirit, as Paul describes them in Galatians, are all relational (Galatians 5:22-23).

Love requires an object,
   Joy is seen by others,
      Peace is made between people,
         Patience is shown to others,
            Kindness is given to others,
               Goodness is passed on to others,
                  Faithfulness is in the midst of others,
                     Gentleness is required by others, and
                        Self-control is in every relationship.

God-centered, Christ-following, Holy Spirit-filled leaders must have relationships. A vital relationship with God shows itself in how one relates to others. As the apostle John put it in 1 John 4:20-21: "The one who does not love his brother whom he has seen, cannot love God whom he has not seen. And this commandment we have from Him, that the one who loves God should love his brother also." This kind of "love lived out in relationship" is not just the most essential characteristic of a church planting network, it's also the reason why people join networks.

While presenting at the Exponential Conference Neil Cole asked the question: "What holds you together?" The churches represented there ranged from simple organic churches to mega churches. The glue that held them all together, they said, was relationships.[48] Later, Cole commented that the presence of God is the glue that holds CMA together.[49] Without exception successful church planting networks point to relationships as the "glue" binding their members and enabling their work. The relationships are really a combination of personal support and the invisible presence of the Holy Spirit – it is that combination which forms the glue.

One pastor we know, who has participated in a network in Indiana, comments on how relationship is worth the price of admission for ministry veterans: "My involvement in a network for church planting has enriched me as a leader in my own congregation, honed my vision for the kingdom of God, deepened my love and appreciation for my brothers who are also involved in the network, and reminded me of the urgency of bringing hope to a dying world. While church planting is the joyous end result, the means by which it is accomplished is a reward in itself." While relationship is a primary characteristic of church planting networks, it is not the purpose, just as the pastor mentioned above. Relationship is brought together and bound by the mission of the kingdom of God.

But let's also note this: when relationship is the sole purpose of getting together, the network quickly falls apart. Tom Nebel, director of Converge Church Planting, articulates this concept well: "Relationship without mission, entropy sets in; and mission without relationship, entropy sets in. But if you put these things together, you get sustainability."[50]

His experience has shown that when the group turns inward, the cohesion and viability crumble. But when their groups are focused on the outward-focused mission, church planting, then their relationships grow and they keep momentum as a group. So then, mission puts them together, relationships are the glue that holds them together, and mission is what keeps them together. They are together, nonetheless, and that's the important part.

In 2010, Todd Wilson, director of the Exponential and Exponential Conference and others, commissioned a study of all the church plants in the greater Washington, D.C. area, focusing on the survival rate of churches and church planter health. Out of this study he concludes that, "one of the single biggest needs that those three hundred planters have [is] they are lonely, they are discouraged, they feel disconnected, they struggle financially."[51] This study is a wake-up call clearly showing how important decentralized networks and the personal support they can provide is to the mission of planting churches. Wilson notes that "networks are ideally suited to deliver support and encouragement to church planting families in the post-launch phase and that increased emphasis is needed in this area."[52]

Structure of Church Planting Networks

The most central issue in regard to the structure of church planting networks, especially in contrast to the singular isolation of most churches on the one hand and the denominational hierarchy on the other hand, is the movement from centralization toward decentralization. This movement is happening all around the world in various sectors throughout society. Even when looking to significant events in the recent history of America, one will find decentralized networks.

Ori Brafman and Rod A. Beckstrom point toward Al Qaeda's organizational structure, citing the terrorist attack of September 11th on the World Trade Center in their book *The Starfish and the Spider*.[53] After the attack the U.S. government and military had a difficult time combating this terror network because their structure is decentralized. A decentralized network, they claim, not only survives when attacked but can even grow stronger.

They relate the starfish and the spider to two types of organizations.[54] The starfish represents a decentralized organization because it has no head and when you cut off one of its legs, the starfish re-grows the missing leg. When cut into pieces, some kinds of starfish (e.g., the Linckia) regenerate new bodies from each piece.[55] Starfish have no head. Thus, a decentralized organization has no clearly identifiable leader or central hub. The spider, however, has a head and eight legs. It may live without a leg or two, but it won't live without its head. The spider represents a centralized organization.

In the church world, there are typically two types of organizations that plant churches—denominations and networks. Following the analogy, denominations are more spider-like (centralized structure) and networks are more starfish-like (decentralized structure). Notice some of the contrasts between the two and how their description applies to denominations and networks.

Centralized (Denominations)	Decentralized (Networks)
Someone is in charge	No one is in charge
There are headquarters	There are no headquarters
Centralized power structure	Decentralized power structure
Knowledge is centralized	Knowledge is decentralized
Direction comes from the head	Direction comes from the network

As with any broad characterizations, there are wide variations among both denominations and networks. Not all networks are completely decentralized nor are all denominations completely centralized.

Although decentralized organizations have no hierarchy, they are still structured. Amidst the apparent chaos of an unidentifiable leader there is order. Dee Hock, the founder and former CEO of Visa credit card association, spent many years studying, writing and championing the idea of a chaordic organization (chaos and order, together).[56] He defines chaordic as "the behavior of any self-organizing and self-governing organism, organization, or system that harmoniously blends characteristics of chaos and order."[57] This is what is happening, to one degree or another, in church planting networks.

Not all networks are the same. Some are more decentralized than others. John Arquilla and David Ronfeldt describe three types of networks: chain, hub, and all-channel networks.[58] These networks are defined by connections and centralization. The chain network is a series of connected links, connected to only two other links—one in front and one behind. This is decentralized but limited in connection to other links. The next one is the hub network where each link is connected to the others through a central hub. This is more centralized but more closely connected to each link. The third network can be a combination of the two. It's called the all-channel network. Each link is connected to every other link, providing complete communication between all links without going through a centralized hub. It is decentralized and intricately connected.

Church planting networks are a mixture of the chain and the hub networks and none are a pure all-channel network. Neil Cole's Church Multiplication Associates (CMA) is the most decentralized church planting network. Cole uses the following framework to describe it: "I believe Jesus is ultimately building a type of all-channel network that represents His body on earth. CMA is therefore in the process of becoming an all-channel network."[59]

Most of the networks we have studied are neither completely centralized nor totally decentralized. They are a combination of the two. Brafman and Beckstrom label this combination *the hybrid organization* and they call it the sweet spot because the organization gets some of the benefits of being centralized and the benefits of being decentralized without being too compromised.[60] So what does this look like for church planting networks? It depends on the network. They each have a unique structure, but each of them has two scales—macro and micro networks.

The ten networks we include in this book are mostly macro-level networks because they have a national spokesperson and vision. Some have a global presence. Within each of these macro networks there is a localized presence—micro-level networks. The micro-level networks within each organization are almost all geographic specific, either defined by a state, county or city.

Instead of describing the structure of each network equally, we will focus on recurring traits and dominant characteristics of these two types, highlighting a few specific networks along the way. These structures are only as important as they help describe *how people are connected in church planting networks*.

The dominant characteristic of a network is relationship. We classified relationship as the most essential characteristic of networks. Now we want to describe what those relationships look like in various contexts across the Continent. This is merely a snapshot of the history of the church as best we can tell from our research. Hopefully this will only be a starting place from which networks can learn and develop better models.

National Macro Networks

Church planting networks typically have a national or other large-scale presence. Not every network, however, functions on a national or macro-level yet. Some are still growing into a national or even global sense of being. Acts 29, Stadia, New Thing, ARC and others have a national presence. This national presence is often made evident through websites which describe activities of multiple smaller gatherings around the country or through information on different church-planting projects in different states.

The national presence can be seen through the national ministry of network speakers, network conferences (where people from around the country are invited), and especially through annual large scale gatherings of a network. For example, Acts 29 tries to bring their entire national network together for a retreat in the summer each year. The focus of this gathering is relationships. President Scott Thomas describes why people come: "They don't come for the teaching, they come to collaborate and spend time together," Thomas says. "They attend because they like each other, honestly. So it's not a hard sell!"

Stadia has a yearly gathering during the Exponential Conference. Planters room with each other and gather for special sessions with each other. Special gatherings are established just for the wives of church planters. Everyone also comes together on the first night of the conference for their annual celebration. It is hard to find a room big enough for the hundreds of planters, coaches and others who come together to celebrate what God has been doing in networks across the country and in the international places where they are just starting to plant churches.

NewThing leaders often get together more than once a year. ARC, a more centralized network, has a large conference of 1,500 church leaders every year.[61] They call it the "All-Access Conference", offering potential church planters immediate opportunities for relationship with ARC's leaders and current planters.

"The biggest thing ARC has to offer is a church planter's culture," says Billy Hornsby, a national leader and president of ARC.[62] "We all have a vision, we're doing life together, and we work together to multiply manpower, evangelistic efforts and world missions." Connections are made at this large national gathering, which provide the foundation for further ministry among planters. ARC planters are encouraged to develop small "self-coaching" groups of other planters. "They're calling each other constantly," Hornsby says.

Friendships are forged at all-access gatherings and then translate into life-long friends. ARC is the most centralized network because it has the most consistent, well-developed and centralized leadership and national conference. It does not have localized micro-level structure. Even their coaching is centralized, provided by four full-time coaches on staff. This stands in contrast with CMA, which is more decentralized, functioning with a very loose, non-centralized national presence.

Exponential Network is the largest of the national or macro networks. Led by Todd Wilson, this network publishes books and resource material and facilitates connections. The most important national expression of the network is the annual "network gathering" for all church planting networks every April. The Exponential Conference is the national expression of Wilson's vision building a "network of church planting networks."

Local Micro Networks

Most of the high profile networks have a national or macro expression. They are known through national leaders, conferences, books, resources and the like. But for most planters, the deepest connections and life-changing actions occur in smaller network gatherings where people meet face to face and connect person to person. We call these gatherings local or micro networks.

For example, CMA develops relationships through small clusters around the country. Potential leaders attend a "Greenhouse" training to learn about organic church planting, mentoring and developing disciples. Then, they attend a second advanced Greenhouse training a year later. In between the two Greenhouse events attendees gather monthly for prayer and relationship-building. Cole believes this decentralized focus allows greater collaboration and relationship than a more institutionalized approach. "We're dealing with so many different kinds of churches, from Pentecostal to Reformed and everything in between, and yet we're all working together," he says. "It's common to go to a Greenhouse and see these folks not just attending together but teaching the same stuff at the same time. That's unique to our movement and we celebrate that."

The micro-level structure and schedule of meetings will be different in function from network to network. One characteristic of these more localized networks recurred throughout our discussions with these networks--most of whom meet about six times a year. We asked Thomas why it's important to be in a geographically located network. He answered saying,

> You know guys will just hide out . ... So we want them to be rubbing shoulders with and interacting with other guys so they can really call people out on issues of the heart. And they do that pretty regularly. We just really see that as . . . our covenant with each other—we will stand side by side in arms, defending and fighting for our brothers. And we'll do that even if it's uncomfortable for us. We'll confront, we'll rebuke, but we'll also apologize. We will encourage and we'll uplift and we'll strengthen one another as well.[63]

Acts 29 also holds regular meetings for pastors to encourage and support each other. The network's regional directors pull the groups together at least every other month. While their networks are geographically located, they are not primarily centered around a target city or region. Instead they rally around leaders. Every member church of Acts 29 is required to be in one of these regional networks, in addition to any other connections they may have, as the regional one is the micro-network where the leader personally knows the men under his care. Here's how Thomas describes it:

> We don't want to the guy in Florida to say—*here's a way I can hide, I can be connected to* [a] *Soma church (out West) because I connect with the guys are out West. So I won't have to mess around with these guys here in Florida.* That's not true. He has to be involved with the guys in Florida—we want them examining his life, being in his life, knowing what's going on, on a regular basis, just from a practical standpoint.[64]

Similar to CMA and Acts 29, the Stadia, Vision360, Converge, Launch, and NewThing networks have clearly defined, active and multiplying micro-level networks throughout the country.

The San Diego Church Planting Alliance (SDCPA) is unique in our survey as it is the only network which operates solely on a regional scale. As their name suggests, they are an emerging network that plants churches in San Diego. Their vision is massive and they are gaining ground quickly, focusing on one specific geographic community. We want our readers to know about this network because it provides us with a model that could be expanded to many North American cities.

The SDCPA wants to double the number of Evangelical churches in San Diego County, raising the number to 1,600 churches by 2025. We have never seen anything like that. Church leaders in San Diego have been meeting since Fall of 2010 to discuss what their network will ultimately look like. While their focus is on San Diego County, they have a global vision. They desire to have a worldwide impact; their methodology, however, is localized. John Worcester, the coach of the SDCPA, says, "We believe that the best way to win someone to Christ is to bring a healthy new church right to the doorstep. It's speaking their cultural language . . . but that's not to the exclusion of the nations."[65] This means that when they want to plant a church, they try to look first to the people in their local congregations, the churches in San Diego County.

The other intensely regionally-focused network is Vision360. They have a very strong emphasis on cities as micro-level networks. In fact, one of their defining characteristics is city-centricity. Vision360 focuses on each micro-network taking "spiritual ownership for the region." In other words, for Vision360, they emphasize and value "place." This emphasis is evident in their mission "to serve and empower a collaborative church planting community in five hundred global cities by 2025."[66] They are currently active in ten cities across the country with anywhere between a full-blown organization in one location to another one that is just starting. They refer to themselves as the Switzerland of the Kingdom of God, providing neutral ground upon which people can freely operate. For this reason their structure is determined by the specific cities and the people with whom they collaborate and connect. In this way Vision360 functions on the regional level that looks different in various locales.

Launch is a relatively new network but it has a national vision for micro-networks. Launch has hubs around the country, each of which has an anchor church. Launch network leader, Mac Lake, defines these micro-network hubs as "a region that's large enough to have a collection of church-planting churches working together as launch partners that is small enough to maintain relationship." Typically it is a two-hour radius around the city. They have hubs in Jackson, Mississippi, in Atlanta, Georgia and in Winston-Salem, North Carolina, and they are talking to other cities about joining Launch.

Launch provides local networks where leaders gather together for a two-fold purpose: to continue the leadership development process and to connect people for the purpose of church planting. These are often best-practices sessions. "Networks should never plant churches," Lake says, "Churches should plant churches."[67] Launch does not want to cripple a church's ability to reproduce. They put people in the hubs to get them locally involved in church planting. The hubs can plant within or outside of their region but ideally they will plant in their own region.

NewThing has fifteen regional networks and each planter receives monthly coaching, feedback and ongoing relationship with other planters from the network in their area. For Dave and Jon Ferguson, brothers and co-founders of the network, the importance of these relationships began at home: "We grew up in a family with an attitude of 'you can do anything,'" Dave says. "So a huge part of the culture at our church and with the network is an assumption that other people are up to something good. We want to give them opportunities and equip them to go for it."[68] Dave's positive, forward looking attitude is infectious.

This relational culture permeated the church's first small groups—which quickly multiplied—and continues to influence the network's relationships. "It's a fascinating thought," Dave says, continuing Thomas's reflections on the next generation's need for mentoring.[69] "Maybe part of the key to making this whole thing work is growing healthy families."

Stadia currently has active micro-networks in over twenty states – and we hope to develop them in every state. In the second half of the book we will describe the Stadia story, but for the purposes of this chapter we think it is important to note that we did not start out with a network focus. We quickly made the shift, however, when we learned that relational connections and shared decision making in a micro-network environment is the most effective means of supporting current church leaders and planting churches.

Being a denomination, Converge stands out from the other networks because it has a dual role. Under the leadership of Tom Nebel, Gary Rohrmayer, and Paul Johnson, Converge was able to plant so many churches through their networks that they doubled their number of churches during a recent twenty year period. Converge's micro-networks utilize 24-Hour LEAD (an acronym for Learn, Encourage, Achieve, and Dream) team gatherings for relationship building, coaching, and church planting. These effective 24-hour gatherings for pastors and church planters include time for study, goal-setting and just having fun together.

These small groups of 6-10 pastors meet six times a year to *learn* from one another through discussion and application of resources, to *encourage* spiritual health by sharing struggles, to pray together and enjoying fun activities, to *achieve* shared goals by accepting responsibilities furthering the mission and to *dream* about expanding God's Kingdom.

45

"The LEAD team includes training and brainstorming, but what really keeps the guys coming back is the encouragement," says Gary Rohrmayer, Converge Church Planting's associate director. "We have a nice dinner together and enjoy a fun activity—LEAD teams have done everything from bowling to laser tag."[70] Relationship is the glue that holds networks together, especially on the micro-level. They have eleven regions across the US, each of which has a regional director who is full time and funded autonomously by their regional association.

Because LEAD team members also bring different skills to the team, new planters receive the benefit of wide-ranging wisdom. Nebel and Gary Rohrmayer, Converge Church Planting's national associate director, use a Mayo clinic analogy: "It's the idea of specialists. It's one thing to see a doctor; it's another to see a group of doctors with different specialties. We believe there are lots of church planters who could have planted a healthy church but crashed, and who could have succeeded if they had worked in a collaborative network."[71] Each member plays one or more roles based on his giftedness ranging from spiritual formation to fundraising to recruiting new planters. The 24-hour LEAD team meetings include time for each participant to report on his progress. We have found these meetings to be so effective that Stadia has now adopted them as a common practice. The last chapter of this book describes these gatherings in detail.

Conclusion

We think it is important to have presence on both a macro-level and micro-level network level. The approaches vary from network to network. On the micro-level most of the networks have a presence, some highly structured, consistent and organized, while others function more organically by adapting to the regional needs and what is already going. We believe personal relationships, typically the micro-level relationships, are the most important relationships of all. Staying connected in this way gives leaders face-to-face interaction so they encourage one another, learn from one another and plant churches together. There are various means of keeping connected to each other, and we will address these in the chapter on *koinonia* and sharing kingdom resources.

4

CATALYTIC LEADERS AND COACHES

In this chapter:
- An introduction to "apostolic leaders" and their role in networks
- An introduction to local network coaches and what they do to activate church planting

Leadership is challenging. Leaders are often not sure what to do or say to help people understand. You may have heard the story about David Garrison when he described how the internet functions. He couldn't take it anymore, so he stood in front of a group at a top hotel in Paris, France, and lied to them: "I said *I* was the president of the Internet."[72] He was asking them to invest in what was then a new entity—the World Wide Web. He had been hired to raise funds for Netcom which was "an early Internet service provider (ISP) like AOL or Earthlink."[73]

Garrison faced various challenges. The "best part," he recalls, "was the situation with the investors in France in 1995 described above. They shared a common problem with most people that year: they didn't know much about the Internet." Dave's job was not only to explain the Internet but get them to invest financially. They wanted to know who the president of the Internet was but as we commonly know today there isn't one. They didn't understand. Dave tried to explain that the Internet was a network of networks, even up to forty thousand networks, but to no avail. They asked, *"Who decides? Who's the leader?"* He couldn't satisfy them unless he conceded to their need for one centralized leader so he lied to them admitting, "I was the first president of the internet."

We tell this story because church planting networks, as they exist now, are a new movement in the United States. They can confuse people in a similar way as the Internet confused the potential investors. Not only will networks create a certain amount of confusion—because they are still forming and being defined—but they also have a similar nature to the Internet which elicits similar questions: *"Who is the leader of church planting networks? Who is in charge of them?"* The answer is not simple. Ultimately, no one is in charge but networks always have leadership.

We empathize with Garrison in his struggle to articulate the leadership of a decentralized network. Many of these networks (perhaps all) have not fully established their leadership structure. In this chapter we will explain the major leadership roles in networks as they currently exist.

While some local or micro networks may be spontaneous and without formal leadership, as a general principle, networks rise and fall on leadership. Seth Godin believes the same thing about networks. What we call a network (generally speaking), he calls a *tribe* which he defines as "a group of people connected to one another, connected to a leader, and connected to an idea."[74]

In the last chapter, we talked about the connections between people in the *tribe* (which is similar to a *network*). "Tribes need leadership," Godin says. "Sometimes one person leads, sometimes more."[75] Likewise, church planting networks need leaders—networks are people connected to other people and ideas—someone who will harness the energy or provide coaching or give direction or lead with passion and provide movement.

We see at least two essential leadership roles when it comes to initiating healthy church-planting networks: apostolic leadership and network coaching. Each plays a vital role in accomplishing the mission. The simplest definition of each role are these: *apostolic leaders extend the gospel* and *network coaches connect people together.*

Sometimes in a hierarchical organization, leadership is positional—people are given a position and title so the person can affect change from the top down. Networks, however, are different. Leaders may have a title, but not because someone gave it to them; it's because they are influential. Leadership in church-planting networks is influence--pure and simple. That's what apostolic leaders and network coaches do—they influence people. "The true measure of leadership is influence," as John C. Maxwell says.[76] This is especially true in networks.

Apostolic Leaders

The term *apostolic leadership* comes from the New Testament. The early church had Apostles. Jesus appointed these men during his ministry, "designating them apostles—that they might be with him and that he might send them out to preach" (Mark 3:14). In the book of Acts, Luke makes it clear that these Apostles were given the message of the gospel, the good news of Jesus, in order to take it to the nations. The great commission has an apostolic thrust: *go and make disciples of all nations.* The Apostles took this message to the nations, extending the gospel to and contextualizing the gospel for new regions. After their faithful witness to this gospel, the Apostles eventually died, but their function for the church did not.

At this point, we want to suggest a distinction between the original Apostles and apostolic leaders today.[77] The twelve Apostles (and Matthias) had two qualities, the combination of which characterizes no leader today: they walked with Jesus during his earthly ministry and were clearly chosen by God as Apostles to provide a foundational work in establishing the church (Ephesians 2:20). "Therefore it is necessary," Peter said, "to choose one of the men who have been with us the whole time the Lord Jesus went in and out among us, beginning from John's baptism to the time when Jesus was taken up from us. For one of these must become a witness with us of his resurrection" (Acts 1:21, 22; cf. 1:26).

The Apostles were all chosen by God. Jesus prayed all night before he appointed the twelve Apostles: "One of those days Jesus went out to a mountainside to pray, and spent the night praying to God. When morning came, he called his disciples to him and chose twelve of them, whom he also designated apostles" (Luke 6:12-13). So whether through his Son or through the casting of lots (in the case of Matthias), God chose every Apostle.

They were apostles in a sense of *super-Apostles.* We think there is merit among those who suggest that we have lower-case "a" apostolic leaders who function in a similar role except that they were not foundational to the church and they were not alive with the incarnate Christ. Paul, an Apostle abnormally born, writes about apostolic leaders in Ephesians chapter four:

> It was he who gave some to be *apostles*, some to be prophets, some to be evangelists, and some to be pastors and teachers, to prepare God's people for works of service, so that the body of Christ may be built up until we all reach unity in the faith and in the knowledge of the Son of God and become mature, attaining to the whole measure of the fullness of Christ. (vv. 11-13)

Writing to the church, Paul designates five major functional roles in the church, one of which is this general type of apostolic gifting. An apostle in this sense may be someone who is "sent" to a region or a nation (or beyond). They have a ministry which is not confined to a local church.

Why do we propose that Paul was addressing those beyond the Twelve in this passage? The context of Ephesians points toward that understanding. In his well-known commentary Markus Barth says that Paul's description of the church in Ephesians is different from any other New Testament book.[78] The church not only receives more prominence in Ephesians, but the church is not as localized—in terms of houses and district churches—as in other letters. Unlike Paul's usage of *church* in the letters of Galatians, 1 Corinthians, and Philippians, his usage in Ephesians describes the universal Church. He never mentions any names or specific issues in Ephesus. Also, many scholars believe it was a circular letter, intended for the region, not just the Ephesians.

This is important for our discussion because it makes Paul's description of the five-fold ministry functions in Ephesians not limited to one time or place. His letter is about the church in general, so when the goal of the apostle is to build up the body of Christ, this role applies to the whole body of Christ, the universal church. For this reason he does not seem to be referring to merely twelve men; rather he seems to be referring to a function that applies to the church as a whole, beyond chronological or geographical context.

Furthermore, other passages in the New Testament describe individuals with the apostolic role and they were not among the original twelve. The Greek word for apostle (*apostolos*) is used eighty times in the New Testament. While most of these occurrences refer to the twelve, other individuals are clearly designated by the word *apostle* who were not one of the twelve: Barnabas in Acts 14:14, Epaphrodites in Philippians 2:25 (translated "messenger" in the NIV), Silas in 1 Thessalonians 1:1 (and 2.6), Apollos in 1 Corinthians 4:9 (see also 4:6, 3:22, and 3:4-6), and even Jesus in Hebrews 3:1. It's also possible that Andronicus and Junia (Romans 16.7) were apostles, depending on how you interpret the Greek –either "well known *among* the apostles" or "well known *to* the apostles." These are important passages because they point to apostles as men sent beyond the local church – to take the gospel to new regions and expand the kingdom of God beyond the local church.

What does an apostolic leader do in the church today? Alan Hirsch writes about apostolic leadership in *The Forgotten Ways*, commenting about the nature of this kind of apostle and the mission of God:

> I can find no situation where the church has significantly extended the mission of God, let alone where the church has achieved rapid metabolic growth, where apostolic leadership cannot be found in some form or another. In fact, the more significant the mission impact, the easier it is to discern this mode of leadership.[79]

The church needs this type of "rapid metabolic growth" in North America, as we have shown, and apostolic leadership is integral in achieving it. Alan Hirsch defines the apostolic leader's primary role:

> Apostles extend the gospel. As the "sent ones," they ensure that the faith is transmitted from one context to another and from one generation to the next. They are always thinking about the future, bridging barriers, establishing the church in new contexts, developing leaders, networking trans-locally.[80]

We like this definition. Based on it, we believe the primary function of the apostolic leader in terms of their relationship to church planting networks is in *extending the gospel beyond a local region or church.*

We have found two primary types of apostolic leaders in church planting networks: macro-level apostolic leaders (who have a national or global influence) and micro-level apostolic leaders (who have a regional influence). They function similarly but influence others on differing scales.

Macro-level Apostolic Leaders—National or Global Influence

Macro-level apostolic leaders influence church planting on a national or global scale. These leaders raise awareness of church planting across denominational and even international lines. Just as Paul feared neither the spotlight nor the hardship that often comes with leading, apostolic leaders are not threatened by other leaders and are willing to take arrows as they advance the mission.

Using both spiritual and personal authority, apostolic leaders also guard the churches from heresy and guard the truth as they contextualize the gospel in new areas. In his *Biblical Leadership Commentary*, Dr. Bobby Clinton notes that these leaders "challenge traditional approaches to ministry, exert influence to maintain existing churches, and intercede in prayer for these churches."[81]

In the past fifteen years networks like NewThing, Church Multiplication Associates and Acts 29 have emerged as leading church-planting organizations in North America. Unlike denominational structures with huge resources and momentum, these networks have sprung up without significant funding or support, inspired by the vision and passion of an apostolic leader. Although several of these leaders pastor large congregations, they realize the best use of their giftedness is the expansion of the church into new geographical areas and ideological paradigms.

The apostolic leader is the man who inspires the network, not only by drawing people in, but also providing teaching, direction and transmission of the network's DNA. In their book, *Exponential*, Dave and Jon Ferguson articulate three abilities of an apostolic leader: 1) to see the future clearly, 2) to start new things, and 3) to embed and guard truth.[82] From core values to high-level strategy, the apostolic leader pioneers new ground, communicating not just the gospel mission, but also the unique expression of mission in the local church.

It is impossible to understand networks without understanding this leadership role within a network. To help us, we want to highlight three macro-level apostolic leaders: Dave Ferguson, Neil Cole, and Mark Driscoll. These men influence the Church on a national and even global scale.

Dave Ferguson helped plant Community Christian Church (Community), a multi-site church in the Chicago, Illinois, area in 1989. While he continues to serves as the lead pastor, he's also the primary apostolic leader for NewThing Network. The church has birthed twelve additional locations and each leader—from small group facilitators to campus pastors—continuously identifies and raises up apprentices. Ferguson has been a catalyst for the movement by casting vision, sending people out and training new leaders.

Neil Cole is also an apostolic leader and co-founder of Church Multiplication Associates (CMA). In addition to his role, he has worked closely with four other leaders since the late 90s—leaders who are each gifted in one of the areas identified in Ephesians chapter four. "Of our core group, I'm the apostolic leader," Cole says. "Dezi Baker is prophetic, Ed Waken is the evangelist, Phil Helfer is the shepherd or pastor, and Paul Kaak is the teacher. I am a much better person and CMA is a much better movement because all five of us have been together."[83] They have a representative for each of the five roles in the five-fold ministry model in Ephesians chapter four.

Cole demonstrates his leadership and gifts in more ways than one. In addition to launching the network, he helped champion the concept of *organic church*, having written a book by the same name. Organic church is "not a model but mindset," he says.[84] His model exemplifies one aspect of apostolic leadership—breaking new ideological ground. He's not the only one to believe in and advocate this type of mindset, but his calling from God gives him apostolic influence which impacts people on a trans-local level. He won't call himself an *apostle*, but he will call himself an *apostolic leader*, quipping, "I have the frequent flyer miles to prove it."[85]

When we talked with Scott Thomas, president of Acts 29, we asked him about the necessity of apostolic leaders. We asked him if it is possible to have a movement without one of these leaders. He told a story about a time he consulted a small denomination. They said:

> "We want to do what Acts 29 is doing and we want to do it as Mennonite Brethren, but here's our challenge—we don't believe we have a leader like that, we don't have that guy. We have good leaders, but we don't have the apostolic (they didn't use that word), so can we in fact pull this off?" And I would like to say the apostle of apostles is Jesus Christ, and that he's in the midst of it. ... God uses men, he uses (Matt) Chandler, he uses (Mark) Driscoll, guys like (Dave) Ferguson, he uses leaders but I don't know that he's dependent upon them.[86]

So we pressed him further, asking the question, "Would you say that a healthy network must have one of those leaders?"

> I'm not aware of a network that doesn't have one of those—a good strong healthy network that's reproducing, that's really accomplishing something. . . . We're looking for leaders and then we build a network around them. . . men who have His heart who [God] can take and mold and shape and he can build something around. It's ultimately God, it's not the man. God makes the man.[87]

One of those men whom God has used in the Acts 29 network is Mark Driscoll. He is a macro-level apostolic leader, influencing a movement around the nation and the world. Thomas told us that Mark Driscoll's sermon podcasts were downloaded 10 million times last year. "That creates a huge fishing pool," Thomas says. "You can't listen to Mark Driscoll, Matt Chandler, or Darrin Patrick very long before you hear about Acts 29. These guys are the lightning rods, the catalysts to bring attention and direction to the network."[88]

Using this level of influence to point toward Acts 29 is just one way Mark Driscoll exemplifies the apostolic leadership style. From his role as pastor at Mars Hill Church in Seattle to his ongoing involvement as co-founder of Acts 29, Driscoll has attracted thousands of young leaders and inspired them to consider church planting.

Like Thomas said, it's about God and what he does in these leaders. They can't do it alone—they are still team players. For one thing, the focus on mission means another team member or group must do the work of maintaining, implementing and sustaining vision. This reality reinforces the Ephesians four description of separate yet equal gifts. A network with only an apostolic leader will dream big and accomplish little. The apostolic leader must have a team of colleagues.

As noted previously, Neil Cole leads with a group of men with various gifts. Scott Thomas provides day-to-day leadership of Acts 29 and Dave Ferguson relies on his brother Jon, as well as his assistant, Pat Masek, and Eric Metcalf (the director of NewThing). Effective apostolic leaders are team players.

It would be a mistake to think of apostolic leaders at just a national level. Many others have similar roles but on a more geographically specific scale. We call these leaders micro-level apostolic leaders.

Micro-level Apostolic Leaders—Regional Influence

While only a few of the networks we've studied have one clearly identifiable macro-level apostolic leader, most networks have regional apostolic workers. They may not use the same terminology but based on our definition they serve as catalysts for extending the gospel through church planting efforts in their area beyond just the local church.

Typically, these leaders have a vision for their city or state. The Kingdom Synergy Partnership is a network of churches that have come together to plant churches in Ohio, first as a large state-based network and now by utilizing local micro networks within the state.

The KSP network provides a great example of a micro-level apostolic leader. His name is Greg Nettle. He is the senior pastor of River Tree Christian Church and he felt led by God to reach his state. He came up with a slogan which typifies his vision in partnering with other church leaders. Their goal is to "make it hard to go to hell in Ohio." It is a simple statement, but it represents the profound vision to exponentially expanding God's Kingdom through synergy partnerships relentlessly committed to multiplying healthy growing churches.

Under Greg's leadership the vision of KSP is to "exponentially expand God's Kingdom." To accomplish this goal Greg has led his church to sacrificially set the example of planting churches in Ohio. The church typically commits fifty-thousand dollars to a church planting project and then asks other partner churches to stretch for the cause as they have and make financial commitments according to their abilities.

Greg initiates the statewide network gatherings every two months and leads the planning and discussion. At the center of Greg's leadership are the values of KSP: generosity, collaboration, authenticity and urgency. Greg is highly respected for this "apostolic leadership" and through many church plants and local networks, Greg is making it harder and harder for people to "go to hell in Ohio."

NewThing Network has fifteen micro-level apostolic leaders throughout the United States whom they call *regional directors*. They are church planters and full-time lead pastors of growing churches who volunteer additional time for this regional role. Their work includes monthly phone conferences, relationship-building and identification of potential campus pastors and church planters. These fifteen catalysts—and the apprentices who will learn from them—are key to NewThing's vision for a movement of reproducing churches.

Vision360 has a strong emphasis on regional apostolic leaders. They have five positions for every city in which they are working, one of which is a clearly identified apostolic leader called the "city visionary." Steve Andrews, pastor at Kensington Community Church, Troy, Mi., is one of these apostolic leaders for Vision360. As a city visionary, he has two responsibilities: 1) "convening the church (the big "C" church in the city) and 2) casting vision for planting all kinds of churches for all kinds of people," Nick Boring told us.[89] People gather around Steve Andrews. When he asks people to show up, they show up. He is a leader with a lot of influence.

Converge Worldwide, a denomination that functions as a network, has a regional director for each of their eleven regions in the U.S. who is full time and funded autonomously by their regional association. For Converge they have broad apostolic leadership on the geographical level. They have local apostolic leaders but not one identifiable, national apostolic leader. "Right now we're at the beginning of reinventing what the next pool of apostolic leaders is going to be," Nebel says.[90] "We had a mechanism which we called a *church planting think tank*. An apostolic leadership role was adopted (without the title as we now use it) by many of the current leaders back when they were in their twenties. Now those same leaders are asking, "*Who are going to be the vision drivers for the next step?*" We have faith that God will raise up leaders who will go on to be the next regional directors for Converge Church Planting, their church planting movement in the U.S. If apostolic leadership is truly a "God-gifting," as we believe, these leaders can't be raised up, only assisted and protected as they learn to fulfill their God-given roles.

Acts 29 has network leaders all around the country leading their "network of networks."[91] They have networks gathered around apostolic leaders in Phoenix, Nashville, Manhattan, New Hampshire, Las Vegas and Minneapolis plus other places. While the micro-level networks have a geographical locality, they cluster around the leader, not the place: "We don't look for geography, we look for the guy," Thomas says.[92]

Neil Cole tells the story of Kevin Rains who is a great example of an apostolic leader. No one realized Kevin's gift until Vineyard Central Church could no longer use the facility they had been using:

> They were a typical Vineyard church meeting in a community center, planted out of the Cincinnati Vineyard where Steve Sjogren was the founding pastor. And on a Friday, the community leaders came to them and said listen, "This is your last Sunday." So they had one day to figure out what to do without having a space to meet. The pastor's name is Dave Nixon—he got up and told everybody, "Let's move all the chairs . . . meet on this side of the room, if you're on the east side of town, meet on this side of the room, if you're on the south side, this corner and the north side over here." So they split up the congregation, [into] these four groupings. And he said, "Look around and find someone who has a house big enough. Who loves kids? Who plays guitar? Who's a leader? This will be your church until you hear from us otherwise." And they were forced into becoming a network of four

churches. Now that doesn't guarantee DNA. What happened was that one of these groupings had a leader that was truly apostolic. His name is Kevin Rains. And this house church not only had this fresh, vibrant life and DNA, but it began to multiply. Dave Nixon is a humble man who loves Jesus and listens to Him and saw this leadership. ... So he asked Kevin to take over the primary role of apostolic leader for the network, which was not Dave Nixon's gift. To this day, Kevin Rains is the apostolic leader and Dave Nixon works beside him. Truly an awesome story.[93]

The church ended up buying a Roman Catholic Church facility in town and turning it into a multi-purpose building for monthly church gatherings, art shows and CMA training. Cole continues:

They have art shows in there, they have council meetings in there, and they bring their whole network, maybe some twenty churches in the Cincinnati region, together quarterly for a get together and training. They are an organic network. They were the third Greenhouse we ever did, in this Roman Catholic cathedral. Kevin Rains has become one of our trainers. And he felt like it wasn't hitting his values for him to be paid and supported by the church so he gave up his salary and took over his father's auto shop business. He's so apostolic that he franchised it. And he's either retired or about ready to retire now to devote himself to church planting. He's actually making better money doing what he did out in the business world than what's he's doing in the church. So this is a very healthy and strong network in Cincinnati.

While every healthy network has apostolic leaders, not every network has developed them or had enough time to do so yet. Launch, for example, which started in 2010, doesn't have a well-defined group of apostolic leaders. Mac Lake functions in that role right now but he believes they will have a group of these leaders in the future. He called himself the "Launch evangelist," casting vision for the network and recruiting churches to join. In this way he is developing into the role of a macro-level apostolic leader.

It's not just apostolic leaders that catalyze a church planting network though. Network coaches contribute as well. These two roles sometimes overlap. An apostolic leader establishes and protects a particular ideological DNA, expands the gospel into new areas and forges the way of a movement into regions, states and even nations. A network coach, on the other hand, is not so much focused on innovation as on collaboration and local action. A network coach is a catalyst, a person who acts as a coach, recruiting and connecting people for the purpose of church planting.

Network Coaches – Local Influence

Network coaches do not create new structures, start new works or develop the network's macro-strategy, as the apostolic leader does. Their role is not to determine the network's core values or construct a fresh new vision for the future but to rally people behind the already-established vision of the movement.

As Ori Brafman and Rod Beckstrom write in *The Starfish and the Spider*, the catalyst is not the CEO in charge.[94] In fact a catalyst takes a posture of asking questions and drawing ideas out of people instead of directing or telling people what they think. This is a decentralized, non-hierarchical leadership model and for this reason the catalyst is essential to a strong decentralized network. While the apostolic leader crafts the vision and determines the mission, catalysts equip network planters to come together, commit themselves to the mission and eventually launch and lead churches that embody these values. With the DNA of the network as the foundation, they draw the group together and empower it for action.

12 Characteristics of a Network Catalyst
The Starfish and the Spider[95]

1. Genuine interest in others - asks questions of others because they really want to know
2. Loose connections - able to connect and network with up to thousands of people
3. Mapping – naturally see relationships between different groups
4. Desire to help - eager to collaborate even if it doesn't directly benefit them
5. Passion - has an intense drive to achieve goals
6. Meet people where they are - relates with people in their current situation
7. Emotional intelligence - leads with emotions even though highly intelligent
8. Trust - believes in the people and system of the network
9. Inspiration - is not just a collaborator but a motivator as well
10. Tolerance for ambiguity - satisfied when not being able to give definitive answers
11. Hands-off approach - able to get out of the way and let things happen
12. Receding - leaves once the network is catalyzed

Although the catalysts identified by Brafman and Beckstrom work for a variety of non-profit and for-profit organizations, the traits apply equally to coaches in church-planting networks. Like their secular counterparts, the best church-planting catalysts balance sincere interest in others and a desire to help with an ability to step back and allow the organization to grow. They listen and facilitate discussion, they assist without controlling and they multiply enthusiasm without needing the credit.

Here is a description of a catalyst which fits the profile of a network coach: "The catalyst provides the drumbeat for a decentralized organization," Brafman and Beckstrom write.

Because it can't draw upon command-and-control to motivate participants, it needs a strong and ongoing ideology to keep them going. ... Catalysts are inspirational and collaborative; they talk about ideology and urge people to work together to make the ideology a reality.[96]

This job description may seem overwhelming but several church-planting networks have identified catalyst roles, developed strategies around their leadership and even "coached the coaches" to make them more effective. These leaders definitely serve as catalysts for growth in the networks they serve.

Stadia

Stadia invests significant time and financial resources in network coaches. As a former network coach for Stadia, I (Bobby) can say that our networks are catalyzed based on a coaching system—coaches are expected to build relationships with other leaders in the area, invite them to join together in relationships, cast the vision for church planting and develop a network committed to planting one or more churches. The network coach then helps set up management teams out of the leadership of the network partner churches. The management team in turn finds and hires the church planter.

We have developed a full support system for network coaches, as each coach of a local micro-network receives training and support from the associate directors of church planting networks. The entire system currently receives guidance and support from Brent Foulke, the director of mobilization.

Having worked closely with Bob Logan, the master trainer of coaching in the evangelical community, I (Bobby) have seen the value of his distinction between a mentor and coach: *while a mentor is someone who has gone ahead but comes back and pours in, a coach comes alongside and draws out.* This definition has really influenced Stadia's perspective on coaches. We want network coaches who can convene a group of church leaders and draw out their dreams, their plans and their strategies for planting the church without imposing their own opinions. Stadia currently has network coaches for each of their twenty-two regional networks.

Converge

Converge's LEAD team is a great model to look at in terms of how they develop micro-networks. These teams meet six times a year for study, prayer and relationship. They exist to plant new churches. The network coaches receive a two-day "Leadership Quickstart" training course before establishing their team and they meet with other coaches at least twice a year.

Tom Nebel says about the coaches, "We desire [that they] have apostolic qualities about them."[97] They are influential on a regional scale similar to some apostolic leaders, but their posture is more collaborative than innovative. While they may have a regional influence, their primary gift for a church planting network is to draw people together to catalyze an action plan.

"When people feel heard, when they feel understood and supported, they are more likely to change," the *Starfish* authors write. "A catalyst doesn't prescribe a solution, nor does he hit you over the head with one. Instead he assumes a peer relationship and listens intently. You don't follow a catalyst because you have to— you follow a catalyst because he understands you."[98] This concept of a network catalyst is catching on in our culture. Vision360 has even adopted the word *catalyst* as part of their network terminology.

Vision360

Nick Boring, U.S. Catalyst for Vision360, comes out of the business world where he worked for twenty years in the corporate arena with four different major corporations (including Pepsi Company and General Motors). They wanted to use language for their leaders that non-Christians could easily understand, so four of their five city representatives have *catalyst* in their title. The *city catalyst* is their way of describing a network coach (every network has nuanced variations but the general function of these coaches is the same).

Boring describes this person as the glue that holds the whole thing together, getting initial connections, assessment, training, coaching and a strategic ministry plan going. They are the point persons for the city and liaisons between the micro-level networks in each city and Vision360 as a larger macro-level network. As Seth

Godin says, "No coach, no tribe."[99]   A tribe requires not just kingdom-mission and relationship but leadership as well.

For local micro network coaches to inspire trust, the church leaders in their local network must feel confident in their church-planting experience. The coach typically has a proven track record of success in church planting or a high degree of knowledge about it. He must be able to "identify normal" for the fledgling planter and share helpful insights. The coach should guide a planter to make his own decisions, but this ability requires knowledge of the options.

We end this chapter with the story of Dave Milam, an effective network coach. Dave planted a church in Charlotte, North Carolina in 2004. He has a passion for lost people and a desire to do whatever it takes to reach them. After he established Kinetic Church Dave was naturally drawn into the role of recruiting other local church leaders to join him in planting more churches. Stadia came alongside Dave to provide further training in coaching and in the network process.

Dave was so inspired that he moved from recruiting churches for a local network to drawing in other churches and an evangelistic organization into the network process. Now Dave serves as an avid recruiter for the entire state – drawing leaders into the networks, teaching them about church planting and inspiring them to join with him and others in the relationships of support, and more importantly, for the important mission of church planting. Dave started as a church planter, moved to serving as a local network coach and now he is developing into an apostolic role for the whole state.

Both apostolic leaders and network coaches serve as catalysts to awaken the mission of the kingdom of God in leaders around the country. Jesus prayed that the church would be unified as a testimony to Jesus. Catalytic leaders bring people together and move them together, unifying as Jesus prayed. As Scott Thomas said above, it is God who makes the man. But the man must yield to God's making, as well.

The amazing reality is that just like the church of each age, the church of today has the opportunity to be used by God in new ways. Each network we have highlighted hold to different visions, strategies and goals. These differences make each network unique, stemming from leaders and making up each network's DNA.

5

IDEOLOGICAL DNA AND ALIGNMENT

In this chapter:
- Distinctive ideological DNA of the highlighted networks
- The centers out of which the distinctive DNA of each network springs
- A summary comparison of each network's DNA

So far we have addressed two key elements of a network: relational connection and catalytic leadership. Now we turn to the third key element of church planting networks: ideological DNA. As we mentioned in chapter two, Seth Godin defines a tribe as "a group of people connected to one another, connected to a leader, and connected to an idea."[100] This has served as a framework for helping us understand networks. Without people there is no network. Without leadership the people have no direction and without an idea (or a particular ideology) the network has no cohesion--nothing holding them together.

The order of this sequence is important—the people gather, the leaders catalyze and the beliefs unite. In networks, common ideology does not materialize from thin air—it comes from the leaders. Brafman and Beckstrom note that "ideology is the fuel that drives the decentralized organization . . . Take away ideology, and the organization will crumble."[101] In most networks the apostolic leader is the keeper of each network's ideology and, consequently, the network's DNA. The apostolic network leader embeds that DNA—a unique mix of core values, beliefs, goals and strategies into each new church.

In scientific circles DNA (or *deoxyribonucleic acid*) is central to life—cells of every living thing contain DNA which carries genetic information. When cells multiply each one replicates the DNA and its code, ensuring that new cells look like their source cell. So when we use the phrase *ideological DNA*, we mean that which defines the network theologically or philosophically (ideology)--the code which will be passed on to various contexts within each network.

Ideological DNA sets the course of growth and development for a network. Just as a human body grows from an embryo into a fully grow adult, so networks grow and mature. John Worcester, the leader for the San Diego Church Planting Alliance, believes that churches have stages of growth in their lifespan: [102]

1. Growth to reproductive size (i.e., growing as an individual church)
2. Reproductive years (i.e., resourcing new churches)
3. Grandparent years (i.e., helping adult children with resources and wise counsel)

Not every church grows in this way or in this order, but it is a helpful description for how churches can grow. The same is true of healthy networks so that, just as a church has a distinct DNA, so do church planting networks. Just as the network body grows, the DNA with which it began determines the growth. The face of a network (that which is visible) is largely determined by the DNA.

Using a few different analogies, the trajectory of a flying object is determined by how it is launched. When a missile launches, the calibration of the missile determines where it will land. When a spaceship sets course, every small adjustment affects its route in the atmosphere. When a car travels, the specific roads determine the destination. Likewise, each network has a direction that stems from ideology. This DNA sets the tone for how the organization thinks and acts. Troy McMahon, a church planter, tells a story which illustrates how one church planting network lives out their unique convictions.

Troy McMahon's Story

Troy McMahon is a strong advocate for NewThing, a movement focused on reproduction at every level. His story shows how a network's ideological DNA sets the tone of a movement. We heard the story from both Dave Ferguson and McMahon himself. As we listened to their story, they displayed a strong relational bond to one another but an even stronger devotion to their ideological DNA summed up in their mission: "to be a catalyst for a movement of reproducing churches relentlessly dedicated to helping people find their way back to God."[103]

Dave Ferguson helped plant Community Christian Church (Community) in the Chicagoland area in the late 80s. Since then Community has started over twelve multi-sites in the area and NewThing Network of which Ferguson is a leader, has helped create fifteen micro-level networks across the U.S. "We started Community Christian Church with a threefold vision," Ferguson starts.

> Phase one, we saw ourselves being an impact church; phase two we wanted to be a reproducing church; and phase three, if God would bless it, we wanted to be a catalyst for a movement of reproducing churches. And I'm not even sure we knew what that meant, but we just knew that was probably bigger and more impacting than phase one and phase two. [104]

The DNA of the movement comes from Ferguson's leadership. "I think we're going to shift from being a network to being *networks*," he continues. "If we're serious about catalyzing a movement, it's not going to happen with a single network. We need to create a movement that's going to be led by reproducing leaders that are part of reproducing churches that are part of reproducing networks." It's not always easy to develop a leader and then send him off, but for the sake of the mission, Dave did just that with Troy and Janet McMahon.

Troy came out of the marketplace and joined the Community staff with Dave in the late 90s. He began showing signs of strong leadership skills and became a campus pastor. After he became a campus pastor, he sensed the call to plant a church. This wasn't easy for him because he and Dave were close, having worked together for about ten years—"I loved him and having him around," Dave told us.[105] But he knew that in order to be faithful to what God was calling Troy to do, he had to let go.

So Troy and a team of twenty-five people from Community picked up and moved to Kansas City. They sent some key leaders with Troy, one of whom was a young worship leader named Tommy Bowman and his wife, Jessica, who was a longtime Community member. By chance, Troy happened to see Tommy lead worship at the church. Troy had a sense from God that he needed to keep Tommy in mind. About six months later he asked Tommy to have coffee and talk about the church plant. Troy wasn't sure if he found the right guy, though: "I didn't know if Tommy could lead, I didn't know if Tommy could recruit artists, but one thing I knew was that if the sound guy didn't show up or if the trailer got stolen and all we had was Tommy's guitar, he could lead people into the presence of God. I thought that's a good starting place for a church plant."[106]

Tommy wanted to plant. The same night he committed to Troy, his wife, Jessica, spoke up and said, "I want a part to play." So they discussed how she might play a part in the church plant. She had been teaching high school but she wanted to play a significant role in the new church. After discussing and praying about it, she joined the team as a children and families minister. Jessica has an amazing gift of recruiting and developing leaders, and Tommy ended up having great leadership gifts and worship-leading skills. So in September 2007, Tommy and Jessica moved to Kansas City with Troy. They moved with spiritual and financial support from Community. The story doesn't end in Kansas City, though.

In recent months, Jon Peacock (Leadership Resident at Community), came to the place where he was ready to plant. He had been at Community since he first believed, and now he had gone through the process and was just finishing his leadership residency. He was raised in Roselle, Illinois, and now wanted to go back there to start a new church. He called one of his best friends, Tommy, with whom he had grown up, asking him to be the worship leader for the new plant. It was the same Tommy that had just moved out to Kansas City to plant with Troy a few years before that. He recruited Tommy Bowman to move back to the Chicagoland area to plant a new church in Roselle.

Troy told us of both the joy and the pain of sending Tommy, his wife and their two kids back just a few years after they planted in Kansas City:

> It's very emotional . ... His dad was extremely affirming of me over the course of the last three years, even [about] the fatherly role that I played for Tommy, watching him become a parent and being a part of that one. You know, our staff team is not just, *Hey, we work together*; we do life together, we're very enmeshed, so when you tear at that fabric, when you send something out, it's going to be painful. And it is. Imagine—they're gonna have a second baby, a little girl, and I'm not going to get to watch these two kids grow up. Now the great news is their family is going to participate in more of those (network gatherings) on an ongoing basis that I've got to do over the last few years, but it's still hard. I mean, it's hard to send people out—if it wasn't hard, more people would do it.[107]

Community raised seventy-five thousand dollars through an offering in one weekend to support John and the team. Ferguson set the tone so that the local church and network as a whole have a "sending mindset." It's normal to send and release in the NewThing Network: "That's the ethos, the kind of culture that's being created by these networks—that the value isn't just in expanding but also on extending the kingdom to other places."[108]

This story serves as an example of how leaders set ideological DNA and pass it on so it becomes second nature to the network. In this case the DNA of NewThing, the network which partnered with Community Christian to support the church plants, is to focus on reproduction at every level. This is just one of their distinctive values.

We have identified five key components which comprise the DNA of networks: theology, mission, values, vision and strategy. The leadership and organism reveal the DNA of a network as the diagram below shows. Like the tip of an iceberg, leaders and organization float above the water line, revealing the face of the body below. The tip of the iceberg reflects what is under the surface. The DNA starts with theology at the bottom and then moves up toward strategy at the top.

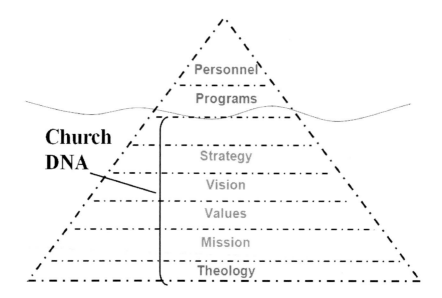

Theological Beliefs

While some networks have denominational affiliations (Converge Church Planting) or explicit statements of faith on theology (Acts 29), other networks are less concerned. Acts 29 displays this commitment in their mission statement (see below)— they are committed to an evangelical, missional and reformed (Calvinistic) approach. All Acts 29 churches and planters must explicitly support these theological beliefs. "We're strong theologically—everything we do is done not from a pragmatic standpoint like *Will it build my church?* but rather from a theological grid," Thomas says, "The first time we look at their application is when they upload their theology. They may have uploaded their resume and references, but we 'pass' them with their theology."[109]

For many of their leaders the theological emphasis and centrality of the gospel, understood from a Reformed perspective, is the most important reason they affiliate with the network. Matt Chandler, lead pastor of The Village Church in Highland Village, Texas, says their theology is the reason why he is an "Acts 29 guy".

Converge Church Planting (formerly the Baptist General Conference) also offers a faith statement as well as position statements on baptism and church membership and resolutions for the denomination's annual meeting. Their theological DNA is self-described as "Baptistic but broad." However, within Converge their micro-level networks sometimes have unique theological grids upon which they all agree.[110]

Missional Distinctives

As we described in chapter one, each network is devoted to the Mission of the Kingdom—to seek and save what was lost. The way this Mission is contextualized, however, depends on the network. The chart below shows a brief overview of each network's mission. The column titled "mission statement" is what they have stated as their general mission or purpose as a network:

Network	Mission Statement
CMA	*"Church Multiplication Associates (CMA)* exists to facilitate church multiplication movements by focusing resources on reproducing healthy disciples, leaders, churches, and movements."
NewThing	"Our Mission is to be a catalyst for a movement of reproducing churches relentlessly dedicated to helping people find their way back to God."
Vision360	"Serve and Empower a Collaborative Church Planting Community in 500 Global Cities by 2025"
SDCPA	"Fill San Diego with healthy, reproducing churches."
Launch	"Inspiring and equipping next-generation planters to lead strong."
Stadia	"Stadia brings people and churches together to transform lives and communities through church planting."
Converge Worldwide	"Our mission is to multiply transformational leaders and churches."
Acts 29 Network	"The Mission of Acts 29 is to band together Christian, Evangelical, Missional & Reformed churches, who, for the sake of Jesus and the gospel, plant new churches and replant dead and dying churches across the United States and the world."
ARC	"We are an association of relational churches working with church planters, church leaders, and churches in transition to provide support, guidance and resources to launch and grow life-giving churches."
Exponential	"We exist to attract, inspire and equip Kingdom-minded leaders to engage their time, talent and treasure in a movement of high-impact, reproducing faith communities."

Each one is explicitly devoted to planting churches. Yet their distinctive mission statements surrounding this goal make them all unique.

Values

Values are typically more distinct than mission for each network. The values build off of the mission, giving specific direction. For example, the Launch Network has decided to focus on leadership and soul care. For Mac Lake, these two aspects of the mission are essential for the success of a church planter and the church plant. When the leader is equipped to "lead strong," the mission will succeed. He says, "When you cut Launch, I want us to bleed leadership."[111]

Church Multiplication Associates (CMA) has seven official values, but they like to focus on their DNA, which is an acronym to describe their core values:[112]

D = Divine Truth
N = Nurturing Relationships
A = Apostolic Mission

These are the elemental aspects of community life for CMA, and they emphasis this DNA at every level of church life, from the smallest unit in their movement (*Life Transformation Groups*) to the largest unit (either a network of organic churches or a single church with a network of small groups).

NewThing, as mentioned earlier, values reproduction on every level. They seek to ground themselves in relationships which nurture development. They ask every church in their network to have residents. They are constantly seeking to develop leaders and resources for their leaders.[113] Their values – as the distinguishing mark of their network – are the "Four Rs"—reproduction, relationships, residents and resources.

Vision

"We all have a vision," says Billy Hornsby of the leadership of the Association of Related Churches (ARC). Hornsby's sense of the vision emerged from a dawning realization that many churches were not reaching their cities for Christ.[114] After Hornsby visited Greg Surratt, pastor at Seacoast Church in Mt. Pleasant, South Carolina, he realized they shared the same vision. Hornsby saw a leader "more concerned about reaching lost people than building his own ministry."[115] This shared vision inspired their commitment to plant 2000 churches by 2025.

Vision360, as one might expect, has a well-defined vision "to follow Jesus, transform cities, and change the world", with a mission "to serve and empower a collaborative church planting community in 500 global cities by 2025." Their vision is to be a glocal church planting movement—global and local at the same time."[116] Their vision is to be a glocal church planting movement—global and local at the same time.

Glocal is a concept Bob Roberts championed in his book *Glocalization: How Followers of Jesus Engage the New Flat World*. Roberts describes the concept:

> Glocal is another term for the flat earth that describes the seamless integration between the local and global, and it is not surprising that this term originated in the East. It was popularized in the early 1990s by Roland Robertson, a sociologist from Scotland and a pioneer in the study of globalization. Leonard Sweet later introduced it to the Christian world.[117]

The concept that Bob Roberts describes is a combination of global and local together. In a sense this term describes how the world is flat—what happens here in one place affects what happens somewhere around the world, and what happens there affects here. The rise of globalization is changing our world, even the way churches function. Roberts says, "In the span of a few years, the information revolution merged with the communications revolution and global business revolution. That puts us all together in the same room for the first time since the Stone Age."[118] Vision360 has taken this into their particular ideology and made it part of their DNA. Currently they are active in ten cities across the country potentially with another four to six cities in the near future.[119]

The distinction between globalization and glocalization is that the former emphasizes the global nature of modern society and the latter emphasizes the local aspect of that globalized society. The San Diego Church Planting Alliance is glocal as well. While they have a similar vision, their strategy for a glocal impact is more localized than Vision360.

Vision is a vital part of networks. The Kingdom Synergy Partnership (KSP), a state network developed in partnership with Stadia, has a simple vision which inspires all that they do – "make it hard to go to hell in Ohio." This vision inspires a sense of urgency that permeates the network and creates a passion to plant churches. Greg Nettle and the KSP leaders constantly remind themselves that the stakes are big--the eternal destinies of people all around them.

Strategy

John Worcester, whom we described in a previous chapter from the San Diego Church Planting Alliance, maintains an explicitly glocal vision which requires a localized strategy. "We believe," Worcester comments, "that the best way to win someone to Christ is to bring a healthy new church right to the doorstep. It's speaking their cultural language . . . but that's not to the exclusion of the nations."[120] The strategic distinction is that local churches in San Diego County are the source for making this happen. The goal is glocal, the method is local. Worcester states, "The best training ground is right in the one church you're in and the guy you're raising up to become the church planter."[121]

The process is somewhat simple—the apprentice starts with cell churches. Once faithfully multiplying on that level, the leader is ready for more responsibility which may lead to church planting locally or globally.

Stadia's strategy is to set up systems for network and planter care. We have found that consistent planter care requires healthy systems. From formal assessments of potential planters and their wives to ongoing coaching, Stadia's systematic approach provides practical help through systematic processes designed to care for planters.

In my role as president, I (Marcus) see the big picture on planter care every day. I know the importance of planter care, from the first moment contact is made through assessment all the way through training, coaching, mentoring, to seeing the planter help plant other churches and learn to care for planters himself. By developing systems, from planter care through to network care, we can best provide a supportive relational environment for planters which brings both health and success. Healthy systems, properly implemented, result in healthy processes and healthy church plants. We advocate healthy systems.

Alignment

Successful networks include all five of these elements in their DNA—theology, mission, values, vision, and strategy—but they may not always emphasize them all. We often find one element in a network's DNA which stands out, becoming central to the other parts of the DNA. Below is a summary of the distinctive element within each network's ideological DNA *from our perspective*. The networks may not use these words or phrases to describe everything they do, but for the purpose of our current study, these may be helpful in discerning differences between each network we highlight in this book. In a word or two here is how we would describe the networks:

Church Planting Networks
Core Distinctives

Network	Distinctive Ideology[122]
CMA	Organic
NewThing	Reproducing Leaders
Vision360	Glocal (globally-focused)
SDCPA	Glocal (city-centric)
Launch	Leadership Oriented
Stadia	Healthy-Systems
Converge Worldwide	Group Support
Acts 29 Network	Theology-driven
ARC	Large Launch
Exponential	Network of Networks

Each core element seems to be the most basic form of DNA and it drives these networks. Understanding these emphases not only helps us to understand each of the networks, it also may help us to look at each network according to their strengths, on their own terms, so that we can learn from them. No one network will have "the best approach."

This perspective may help us see why some people fit into one network more than others. You won't fit in with the NewThing Network, for example, if you aren't committed to "reproduction at every level." CMA is not a great choice for planters who don't support their emphasis on organic, decentralized growth. If a church planter is interested in launching a large Sunday service, then joining up with ARC or Launch might make sense. Common ideology binds a network together, gathering people around a central idea.

Ideas have the power to shake the world around us. As we write, the people of the Egypt are clamoring together, protesting domestic injustices. Newscasters, reporters, and commentators call what is happening in Egypt specifically a *revolution*.

Starting on January 25th, 2011, Egyptians gathered in the streets en masse for "protesting poverty, rampant unemployment, government corruption, and autocratic governance of President Hosni Mubarak, who has ruled the country for 30 years."[123] By February 11th, less than three weeks after protests began, Mubarak stepped down from his position. At first he had made concessions but refused to resign. Eventually, however, the people got their way, chanting "one hand, one hand".[124] They stood united around one central idea—liberation from Mubarak's tyranny. A CBS correspondent reported, "The peaceful Egyptian revolution had a distinct goal, but no clear leader."[125] While they did not have a clear leader, their ideology was succinct—freedom from their ruler. The people of Egypt are changing history.

There is power when people unify behind a central idea. The Apostle Peter calls the believers to whom he writes "a chosen people, a royal priesthood, *a holy nation*, a people belonging to God" (1 Pet 2:9). Christians, as a nation, have the potential to revolutionize the trajectory of North America—not to overthrow our government but to overthrow the tyranny of the Enemy about whom Paul talks in Ephesians as he addresses the believers battle: "For our struggle is not against enemies of blood and flesh, but against the rulers, against the authorities, against the cosmic powers of this present darkness, against the spiritual forces of evil in the heavenly places" (6:12).

While each church planting network rallies around a common ideological DNA, all rally around the person of Jesus Christ, the Word become flesh (John 1:1). We express our unique roles by creating mission statements and organizational strategies, but each network is devoted to the kingdom mission and battle.

We believe that as each network plays a role, moving the Church toward the mission of Jesus, the kingdom of God gains momentum, "and the gates of Hades will not prevail against it" (Matt 16:18). In the next chapter we unpack what this kind of unity can do in the kingdom by describing how networks plant better churches through shared resources. We believe we are better together!

6

NETWORKS AND *KOINONIA*

In this chapter:
- The biblical meanings of fellowship (*koinonia*) and their significance for church planting
- How finances can work in a network
- How planters and other leaders receive training, support, and cutting edge resources

Thus far we have written about the nature of church planting networks. Now we write about the need for support, which church planting networks uniquely provide. In the introduction Mac Lake tells a story of a struggling church planter who planted without the proper support system—not enough people or money. Lake concluded his story by saying, "This should never happen."

Essentially that's why church planting networks exist—so that leaders can plant healthy churches with healthy relationships and support from beginning to end. We say it again—this is the best way to expand the kingdom of God across the dark landscape of North American spirituality.

Through the book of Acts, the gospel message of Jesus brings light into dark places. Even in Ephesus, a spiritually dark place, Paul spoke "persuasively about the kingdom of God" (Acts 19:8). He stayed there for three years "so that all the Jews and Greeks who lived in the province of Asia heard the word of the Lord" (19:10). He cast out demons and healed the sick. People responded, and "in this way the word of the Lord spread widely and grew in power" (19:20).

The Apostles planted churches around the empire as microcosms of the kingdom. As the Apostles took the gospel into new territory, they left behind networks of churches, ones that celebrated a new era in history—the kingdom of God had come and God had changed their lives. The people turned their focus away from their own lives, devoting themselves to Jesus. His kingdom functioned by different rules and one of these kingdom-principles was called *koinonia.*

In this chapter we will take this New Testament concept and re-apply it to church planting. We do this because in a word *koinonia* represents the reason why church planting networks plant healthy churches.

Koinonia is a theologically rich term to describe the transcendent and God-centered bond among believers that inspires them to participate in tangible gospel-work together. Typically translated "fellowship," *koinonia is more than what comes* to our minds when we think of "fellowship." Paul uses it more than any other author of the New Testament, and according to George Panikulam in his book *Koinonia in the New Testament,* Paul's primary emphasis in using this word "is on a Christ centric life", a life of sharing which is evident in various passages. Paul describes the fellowship of the Holy Spirit, the fellowship of Jesus and the fellowship of sharing in Jesus' suffering with this word (2 Corinthians 13:14; 1 Corinthians 1:9; Philippians 3:10).[126]

The bond comes from God but it moves believers together to participate in Christ-centered actions. Acts 2:42 uses this word to characterize one of the primary activities of the early church: "They devoted themselves to the apostles' teaching and to the fellowship (*koinonia*), to the breaking of bread and to prayer." In this context it represents not merely an existential connection but a participatory connection with the body of Christ. It is not an individualistic expression and it's not a word to describe the conversation at a potluck dinner after church. It describes a deep, spiritual bond that causes people to give to one another in various ways.

The essence of *koinonia* is sharing with others what you have received from God. For the early church this often meant giving finances but, as we will see, it meant more than just material contribution. Acts 29's Scott Thomas says, "Collaboration is a kingdom principle and an image of the gospel. We are stewards of Kingdom resources and we must not waste them by doing our own thing. In laying down our personal agendas, God may plant many more churches through all of us."[127]

As we have studied church planting networks in North America, it has become evident that the *koinonia* of the early church characterizes church planting networks today. No other movement that we know of participates in gospel-expansion through shared resources like networks. Healthy networks provide the best environment for successful church planting because they work together, sharing what they have for the advancement of the gospel. They display *koinonia* in the modern context. Networks provide for church plants and church planters with three main types of *koinonia*: financial sharing, planter training, and personal support.

Koinonia and Financial Sharing

The Bible often describes the financial support as fellowship. The root of this concept is the meaning of *koinos,* which is to share something in common. Here is an example in the New Testament of financial contribution as *koinonia*:

> Out of the most severe trial, their overflowing joy and their extreme poverty welled up in rich generosity. For I testify that they gave as much as they were able, and even beyond their ability. Entirely on their own, they urgently pleaded with us for the privilege of sharing (*koinonia*) in this service to the saints. And they did not do as we expected, but they gave themselves first to the Lord and then to us in keeping with God's will. (2 Corinthians 8:2-5)

From the moment he contemplates planting a church to the moment when he makes a commitment to make it happen, the typical planter struggles with this issue, "so many exciting things to do and so few resources". So the planter thinks, *Where's the money? Who's going to help me?* It's nearly impossible to plant a church without the proper resources. Networks provide the resources necessary to plant healthy churches.

In our experience it costs about two-hundred thousand dollars or more to launch a typical multi-staff church with an attractional bent (almost every church plant now also has a missional focus, too). We need to plant around seven thousand churches every year in

North America, as we wrote above, just to keep up with population trends. Although it will not cost two hundred thousand dollars for each of these churches, the financial need to support church planting adds up. Who is going to fund these plants? The answer is the church working together, sharing resources. "Many hands make light work," the saying goes.

Writing about free-market entrepreneurialism, Gary Hamel, Yves L. Doz, and C.K. Pralahad expanded on the concept of sharing with their popular *Harvard Business Review* article entitled "Collaborate with Your Competitors—and Win." They write, "The case for collaboration is stronger than ever. It takes so much money to develop new products and to penetrate new markets that few companies can go it alone in every situation."[128]

The same concept is true for church planting. Church planters must function like entrepreneurs—raising funds, building a team, finding a building. If a leader must do this alone, it is hard work and few churches will be planted, but many hands make light work. The burden is meant for the body of Christ, not one member of the church. In a network a team of leaders joins with the church planter to provide help.

There are various ways to fund church plants. Some networks recruit established churches to support the church planter. The amount of support requested may be established on a case-by-case basis or there may be a set amount that has been established as necessary to partner in the church plant. Established churches who participate in the network may contribute a set amount to the network such as a certain dollar figure given every month.

Some churches who "make a covenant" to be in the broader network may commit to give a certain percentage of their tithes and offerings to North American church planting. In such cases it is common to ask churches to regularly give 2 percent. These same churches often also hold special offerings beyond the two percent for church plant projects that need additional funding.

In some networks the church planter will be asked to pay back the money that was given to him for the church plant out of regular tithes and offerings once the church is started, and then he will be asked to continue to support church planting. Some networks ask all participants for 2 percent of regular tithes and offerings, some ask for 5 percent and some ask for 10 percent for up to ten years after the church has been launched. None of the networks require or extract this money in a top-down approach. Here is how the ten networks we highlight harness the power of financial collaboration:

Network Financial Contribution Structures

Network	Continuous Funding Structure
CMA	No definite structure—many are bi-vocational planters.
NewThing	Micro-level network churches give $5,000 per year to their regional network, and the regional network contributes $10,000 per year to NewThing Network as a whole.[129]
Vision360	Asks church plants to give 5 percent back to the Vision360 city that launches them
SDCPA	Relies on local churches and denominations for church plant funding.
Launch	"Partners" give 2 percent to Launch.
Stadia	Asks church plants to give 10 percent back – 5 percent to Stadia and 5 percent to their own network plants.
Converge Church Planting	No definite structure—some churches give up to 2 percent back to Converge.
Acts 29 Network	Asks church plants to give 10 percent to church planting.
ARC	Recommends to church plants to give 2 percent back to ARC.
Exponential	Connects planters to existing networks. No specific funding of church plants.

It's important to note that these networks are low on control—the approach is not to *require* a certain amount of financial participation because sharing financial resources is an essential element of "fellowship" in the network. The Association of Related Churches (ARC) asks that 10 percent be given back until the money invested in the plant project is paid in full and then 2 percent for an indefinite period – and they ask each church to commit to foreign missions beyond that 2 percent. Launch "partners" give 2 percent.[130] Acts 29 doesn't fund any plants as a network but they ask planters to give 10 percent to church planting in general in a "pay it forward covenant." "We're low on control and high on influence," President Scott Thomas says.[131]

Stadia asks plants to give 10 percent of the regular tithes and offerings back – 5% is given to Stadia for more planting projects and 5% is given to another network church planting project of the planter's choice. Financial strategies like these result in millions of dollars every year for church planting and world outreach.

"The agreement is we plant churches that plant churches that support world missions," says Billy Hornsby.

> We did a survey of how much all the churches had given to missions since they began and it totaled over $40 million dollars. That's a crazy statistic—it totally caught me by surprise. We're giving at a rate of $7 or $8 million dollars a year to plant churches in Zimbabwe, Mozambique and Costa Rica.[132]

Church planting networks are a good investment because the return has exponential potential. When a hundred churches are giving 2, 5 or 10 percent back to church planting, more churches are planted and these churches will continue to fund other churches and so on. When everyone contributes there is a compounding effect resulting in exponential growth. As Stetzer says, "The kingdom is best advanced through multiplication and not just addition."[133]

Not every network is as structured for the levels of financial support found in the ones mentioned above. Converge Church Planting doesn't have a strong funding model on a macro-level, Tom Nebel tells us: "If you're coming and you're looking for a lot of money, you're probably not going to find it in our fellowship."[134] As a whole, they don't fund a church plant because their funding strategy is decentralized. Each of their eleven U.S. regions has a regional director who is full time and funded autonomously by their regional association. "Each region has their own budget and is expected to run their own show," Nebel says.[135]

Church Multiplication Associates (CMA) is decentralized, too. In fact, they don't fund church plants at all. Many of their church planters are bi-vocational.[136] Their organic DNA allows leaders to be funded naturally so that when they've proven faithful and develop a network large enough to support them, they can be paid.

Nick Boring with Vision360 acknowledges the fact that money can be an issue in church planting, but people are much more important than finances for a successful mission. He says that if a church planter had the option of a million dollars or twenty people completely committed to the mission, they would be crazy to choose the money.[137]

As we mentioned in the last chapter, when Troy McMahon left Chicago for Kansas City to plant a church, New Thing sent twenty-five people with him. The San Diego Church Planting Alliance has a creative way to resource with personnel. A volunteer staff is recruited to help new churches. These people go out as "SWAT" teams to new churches for the first few months to help while the church gets established. The SWAT team takes care of things like the nursery, set-up and greeting newcomers. Other networks call these teams the scaffolding people. They are present while the church is being built, but are welcomed back home as returning heroes as the new church develops their own teams.

Koinonia and Planter Training

> When James and Cephas and John, who seemed to be pillars, perceived the grace that was given to me, they gave the right hand of fellowship (*koinonia*) to Barnabas and me, *that we should go* to the Gentiles and they to the circumcised. (Gal 2:9, ESV)

In this passage, Paul describes how he was accepted into the apostolic circle of trust with James, Peter and John. In one sentence (Greek), he connects fellowship with their mission to the Gentiles. The "right hand of fellowship," given to Paul and Barnabas, is syntactically connected with their mission to the Gentiles. In other words missional backing is one element of *koinonia*. Their missional backing stems from *koinonia*, the God-centered bond they received from the other Apostles. In this sense the early leaders supported and sent them out. Networks provide a similar missional backing insomuch that they support planters for mission. This kind of support starts with the church-planter assessment.

Many of the networks we've highlighted provide some type of assessment to discern who has been called by God to plant. This can be a tough process because not everyone passes the assessment, but for those who do the success rate is very high. The assessment acts as a filter through which underlying problems surface. A diverse team of experienced church planters, counselors and other specialists participate during the assessment. In reality the most loving thing church leaders can do is to tell those who have a high probability of failing that, in their experience, it is not a good idea. Likewise it is a great boost for a church planting couple to receive affirmation from qualified assessors that they have the capability to successfully plant a church.

Most assessments last two or three days. Launch has an assessment that is two days long. They have an online assessment tool, which includes a written assessment and a marriage profile. Then, they have a two-day retreat with spouses where a team of professional counselors, Prepare/Enrich-certified pastors and leadership experts assess them. At the end they are in one of four categories: 1) approved, 2) approved with conditions, 2) not yet approved, and 4) not approved. They currently only have one assessment center in Atlanta but they want to select other strategic hubs for developing assessment centers in the future. Many church planting networks use The Church Planting Assessment Center or Team America for assessment.[138]

After assessment most networks provide their own boot camp for training. This is an intensive time of learning where both new and veteran church planters share stories, lessons and resources with the next line of planters. John Worcester of the San Diego Church Planting Association (SDCPA) told us their plan to train up new leaders with both their assessment and boot camp in San Diego.[139] He says that close geographical proximity helps with costs, makes it easier for the spouse to come and opens opportunities for coaching relationships between a veteran planter and a new planter who both live in the same city.

CMA's training is called the *Organic Church Planters' Greenhouse*. "The *Greenhouse* is a relational context for leaders from a city or region to gather together in a supportive environment and learn more about church and church planting from one another and the Scriptures."[140] They have a *Greenhouse* once a week somewhere in the world.[141] While educational training sometimes ends with boot camp-like training, networks are increasingly providing continued training past the initial church-planting launch. After CMA's *Greenhouse* training, in which they teach their DNA (Divine truth, Nurturing relationships, and Apostolic mission), they have monthly follow-up gatherings in the same city or region.[142]

Launch has a similar method of equipping planters. When Mac Lake of Launch planted a church in the 90s, he went to a two-day boot camp. It was purely lecture.[143] When he realized that is how it was going to be, he slipped into the back to talk with another planter. He, like many entrepreneurs, doesn't learn by listening. Since planters function as ecclesial entrepreneurs, Launch makes sure their training is a two-way dialogue.

Inadequate training is one of the top three problems Lake discovered in his investigation of church planting practices as he took over the leadership of Launch. He tried to build Launch with excellence and healthy practices.[144] He explains why this matters so much to him:

> It bothers me because here are these young guys who are in their late twenties or early thirties, taking the biggest risk of their life with their family, they're taking the biggest financial risk of their life and we stick them in a room for two days of their life, dump a bunch of information on them and call it training. And it's not training. It's just dispensing information and dispensing information is not the same as transformation. So if you really want to equip a guy, you have to use an intentional process that is directed towards helping them learn the principles that you're teaching them.[145]

So they developed a new training model that consists of a six-month process in which planters work through twelve leadership lessons-- the twelve Launch leadership competencies.

They reverse engineered successful church planting principles from interviews they conducted with church planters and planting networks by asking the question, *What made you successful?* They turned their answers into twelve lessons and every planter learns them. Planters drive in once a month for an all-day training on a Saturday after already learning the core competency for the session. Each leader may bring this spouse and up to five people from their launch team. They, too, have a regular meeting for continued leadership development and to build relationships between churches for church planting.[146] Each hub hosts these meetings through an anchor church four to six times a year.

Most church planting networks utilize some form of technology for training purposes. Here are some networks that provide educational resources to support planters:

Network	Website
Stadia	http://stadia.cc/
NewThing	http://newthingnetwork.squarespace.com/
CMA	http://www.cmaresources.org/
ARC	http://www.arcchurches.com/
SDCPA	http://sdcpalliance.com/
Launch	http://www.launchstrong.com/
Acts 29	http://www.acts29network.org/
Converge Church Planting	http://www.convergeworldwide.org/
Vision360	http/www.vision360.org/
Exponential	http://wwwexponential.org/

ARC, SDCPA, Launch and Acts 29 put their church planting training online. These and the other networks provide helpful articles, blog entries, books, podcasts and videos. Training is essential for healthy networks because sending a planter out well equipped, and prepared makes for effective new churches.

Koinonia and Personal Support

> When I remember you in my prayers, I always thank my God because I hear of your love for all the saints and your faith toward the Lord Jesus. I pray that the sharing (*heœ koinonia*) of your faith may become effective when you perceive all the good that we may do for Christ. I have indeed received much joy and encouragement from your love, because the hearts of the saints have been refreshed through you, my brother. (Philemon 6-7, NRSV)

Both Marcus and I (Bobby) have planted churches and have walked alongside hundreds of other planters. Our conclusion is that church planting is one of the loneliest vocations on earth. Someone once described it as, "Going to a place you've never been to reach people you've never met for a God you've never seen." While there is some exaggeration in that statement about the difficulty of planting, the reality is that planters face a grueling task laboring in the harvest fields—the hard, rocky harvest fields.

Articulating the struggle is difficult--planters say things like, "I'm lonely, I need help, and I'm dying here." The personal support of caring for the souls of planters may be the most significant contribution church planting networks make for this type of kingdom work. In our experience, nine times out of ten, when the church planter fails the church fails. As Mac Lake said, "The guys who are throwing out the life preservers are drowning." More important than great resources and adequate training is healthy planter support.

Immediately the question arises, *what does that kind of support for planters look like?* Answering that question is like trying to articulate the anatomy of love—it's impossible. We will, however, do our best to describe some manifestations of how networks give the kind of support that Philemon gave, which "refreshed the hearts of the saints" (Philemon 7).

In the context of the passage as a whole (quoted at length above), it seems that Philemon refreshed the saints by the sharing (*koinonia*) of his faith. From this passage it is evident that *koinonia* includes the spiritual aspects of sharing. When a planter is pouring out his life his spirit needs to be refreshed. Even the Apostle Paul desired this kind of support from Philemon: "I do wish, brother, that I may have some benefit from you in the Lord; refresh my heart in Christ" (Philemon 20).

On more than one occasion we have heard young church planters express their need for this kind of support—for relationships, coaching and mentoring—with words like "I am desperate," "I am starving" and "I need these relationships more than you will ever know." This language reflects the needs and the propensity of young leaders to be drawn to networks. Networks generally provide the context for two main sources of spiritual support: group gatherings and personal coaching.

Group Gatherings

In regard to gatherings of groups of 200-500 people, Neil Cole says, "When people do come together in this size grouping . . . they feel a sense of being part of something that is big. They can have a sense of belonging, much as Lakers fans feel a sense of camaraderie when they see others who have the same T-shirt and team loyalty."[147] In a similar way when networks have large, all-network gatherings, planters experience something special, something that energizes simply because of the magnitude of the event. This type of support gives veteran planters an opportunity to refresh the spirits of young planters through teaching, networking and telling stories from their experience in ministry.

"The only reason we come together is relational," says Hornsby.[148] "We all have a vision, we're all friends, we're doing life together, it's always been that way and we do a lot now as church planters." ARC's annual "All-Access" conference gives new church planters unlimited opportunity to connect with ARC's leadership team.

Tom Nebel, in *Parent Church Landmines*, writes on the value of a trans-congregational gathering for the planter.

> We've researched the risk factors that can derail a church planter, and all these factors are significantly reduced when a group—not just an individual—takes an active interest in the planter's spiritual well being and success. The best families include not just parents but aunts and uncles and cousins—so we prefer to see a number of leaders circling a planter, not just a "parent" church.[149]

He extrapolates the biblical analogy of a family to describe how church leaders can provide a wide base of support beyond just parent churches. The family of God is broad and we should utilize relatives outside of the nuclear family (Gal 6:10).

Gary Rohrmayer and Tom Nebel describe Converge as a very relational network. In regard to their regular LEAD team gatherings, Gary adds, "If there's affinity in the group, you build life-long relationships. And we believe no one should plant a church alone—even the Lone Ranger had Tonto."[150]

Personal Coaching

In addition to the group relationships we have been talking about, every network that we have studied values personal coaching. Bob Logan has written extremely helpful and influential material on coaching (e.g., *Coaching 101*).[151] We mentioned his definition above to help define micro-level network coaches but now we are talking about personal coaching for church planters, usually one to one. Logan describes the reason he cares so much about coaching through a personal narrative of his struggles as a young church planter:

The original vision for CoachNet came in 1977. I was a young, struggling church planter who very quickly came to the startling realization that I didn't have the slightest idea what I was doing. So I cried out to God for help--and as I prayed, I got a vision.

Thousands upon thousands of church planters were standing on the California seashore and God spoke in a loud voice: "Okay, everyone, listen up! Your objective--swim to Catalina Island. Line up, and start at my signal!"

Church planters jockeyed for position as the waves pounded at their feet. Then the starter's pistol fired. As they entered the water, some splashed and floundered. Some sank immediately. Most began to wade gingerly into the waves, with longing glances back at the shore. Only a few made it. Catalina lay shrouded in ocean mist some twenty-six miles away.

As church planter after church planter was pulled into the same undercurrent, making the same fatal mistakes over and over, I became very angry and began asking God questions. "Why aren't there buoys to warn them of hazards to avoid during the swim? Why aren't there lifeboats to rescue those who are going under? Where are the church planters who have completed the swim successfully? Why aren't they returning to tell others how to do it?"

In the midst of my own pain and from the depths of my heart, I cried out to God…"Lord, this isn't right. We're not learning from the successes or failures of others. You are the Builder of the Church. If you teach me how to swim--and if you ever place me in the position to help the others lined up on the shore, that's what I want to do."[152]

His own desperation for guidance and support led him to train many church-planting coaches through the years. Logan defines a coach as someone who comes "alongside to draw out."[153] A coach is someone who comes alongside the planter to offer encouragement, prayer and spiritual support – and help him plant the church that he has been commissioned to plant.

Different networks provide different models of coaching. ARC has a staff of four whose only job is to coach planters.[154] They start coaching six to twelve months before they plant and then continue after the church launches.

Tom Nebel, who has vast experience with coaching and church planters, believes that

> Every church planter needs a coach to help him work his plan . ...
> The lead pastor of the parent congregation should not take this role
> because it can create a conflict of interest. The coach needs to be
> separate from the parent to encourage planter honesty,
> transparency, and independence. The parent can, however,
> provide a stipend for the coach as a way of encouraging a
> deliberate coaching plan.[155]

In the Converge system church leaders in the network come alongside the planter to provide essential coaching—an important relationship which is hard to find outside the context of a church planting network. Not many venues connect leaders on that level.

Mac Lake says, "The heart of Launch is that we don't want to just plant churches; we want to plant healthy planters. We really want to focus on the heart and the health of church planters and their families."[156] Networks support planters by refreshing their spirits. This is done primarily through coaching—the net result is not just reproducing healthy churches but healthy planters as well.

Spousal Support

One of the biggest needs we have discovered through our ministry at Stadia is for spousal support. I (Bobby) can remember the early days when my wife and I set out with our small launch team to start a church. I was not the only one facing a stiff challenge-- my wife was having a hard time, too. She was my partner, my co-minister and my strength.

I still remember the day, shortly after we launched our church when, in an attempt to control our young church, a man in charge of a set up team suddenly resigned, saying that he was not going to help any more until he got his way. I didn't know what to do but when I got up early the next Sunday morning to go and help the now small set-up team, my wife got to the school ahead of me. I could not believe it. There she was in her nice clothes, doing what she could to help. For the next six months she got up and helped every Sunday. This is just one example of how she was my rock during the process.

To help the spouses of church planters Stadia has developed a specialized ministry called "Bloom!" (which we describe in detail in Part Two). This ministry focuses on nurturing and addressing the unique needs of those who support their church-planter husbands.

Koinonia through Technology

The sharing of non-monetary resources is an important element for networks—especially ideas and technology. Twitter is a prime example of this principle.[157] Twitter allows users to learn more about ideas and beliefs of leaders, build a connection to the network and point to new resources for leadership by sending status updates to their followers.

Dave Ferguson leverages the impact of his leadership to over 8,000 twitter followers by posting links to multi-site articles, celebrating new leaders and sharing his life. Those who follow Dave learn a lot about church planting every day. Twitter is an opportunity to promote—in 140 character sound bites—his value for church reproduction and healthy churches.

In his blog, "Ten Reasons I Use Twitter," evangelism expert and CEO of Life Way Resources, Thom Rainer, gives a list of reasons he uses twitter. One of the reasons is that he can represent his organization.[158] In the same article he writes, "As the Roman road system opened the way for the spread of Christianity in the first three centuries, Twitter can be another great opportunity to communicate far beyond what we thought possible."[159]

Networks connect people. Leaders connect people through the sharing of ideas. Technology is opening new ways for leaders to connect people to each other and to the DNA of their network every day.

Some of the larger macro networks have developed Internet resources for the support of church planters. Planters stay connected through various technological means. Some stay connected by conference calls at FreeConferenceCall.com, which allows up to 1,000 participants on a call at the same time, record the conference and archive the conversation for free.

Acts 29 uses a forum called *The City*, which was designed by a Mars Hill member, Zack Hubert, and later purchased by Zondervan. Mars Hill Church (a church) and Acts 29 (a network) both use this forum for dialoguing and communicating with their communities. According to Mark Driscoll, *The City* greatly reduces his amount of emails, opening up more time to be on mission and be with people, which is the goal of utilizing technology.[160]

A helpful new resource for leadership coaching is *Gospel Coach*—a training event, book and website created by Scott Thomas and others.[161] The *Gospel Coach* website serves as a practical tool for coaching and, while it was designed for leaders, the website states, "It can be used to shepherd believers of all stages of their life, maturity, age, and gender."[162] The site includes tools for making plans, keeping accountability, holding meetings, creating discussion, sharing resources and subscribing calendar feeds.

Local micro networks are also powerful tools for the sharing of leadership ideas and support. The relationships of local networks provide a context for the sharing of ideas for established churches and for the church planters who come into the network. Sometimes the leaders share sermons, sometimes books, and sometimes children's ministry curriculum or small group curriculum. As the leaders help each other and the church planters, everyone benefits. Many established church leaders have received new ideas, new practices and entirely new approaches, which greatly benefit their leadership because they were in relationship with each other and church planters in a network.

Conclusion

As we have shown, support comes in various ways for church planting. Planters are directly engaged on a daily basis in spiritual warfare. There's too much at stake to let them go out to battle by themselves. There is an enemy they are fighting and he's ferocious. Our "enemy the devil prowls around like a roaring lion looking for someone to devour" (1 Pet 5:8). Too many have been lost, too many have fallen to the wayside and too many have given up for us not to provide them with the support of a network. They need to participate with us in *koinonia.* The kind of *koinonia* we have been describing expands God's kingdom and brings praise to Jesus.

By this point in the book, many may be asking how networks are different than denominations. Don't denominations provide this kind of support? Yes, in part. But we believe networks can give denominations certain tools to more effectively provide planter support. The next chapter helps us focus on this question.

7

NETWORKS AND DENOMINATIONS

In this chapter:
- Learn about trends with young leaders today and how these trends align with network-thinking
- An interview with Ed Stetzer—one of North America's leading missiologists—about denominations and networks working together

In our experience denominational leaders often have trouble with networks. After dialogue with several national leaders, we knew this chapter on denominations and networks would be important. In August of 2009 I (Bobby) was asked to lead a discussion for a group of denominational church-planting leaders with most of the major denominations in the US. I gave the talk on church planting networks to LifeWay's Church Planting Leadership Fellowship. The discussion turned to the ways in which denominations could incorporate the principles of networks.

In this section we want to share with you some of the things that I shared with those denominational leaders and an interview we recently completed with Dr. Ed Stetzer, one of North America's leading missiologists. We believe Stetzer has unique insight into both networks and denominations; perhaps he is more capable than anyone in North American Evangelicalism to comment on this topic. He wrote an influential cover article on the value of denominations for the magazine *Christianity Today* recently[163] and, other than Todd

Wilson (Exponential), he spends more time with networks than anyone we know.

Culturally Relevant Network Principles for Denominations

With some further developments on my 2009 presentation, here in summary fashion, are what we believe to be the most important network principles for denominational leaders to understand. Some of this material comes directly from our experience with young leaders, some of it comes from listening carefully to my children (who are Millennials) and some of it comes from insightful sociologists.[164] Most church planting leaders seem to resonate with these principles. I believe these have become foundational in the lives of young North American church leaders today. Networks are more suited to these principles, but healthy denominations can find ways to adopt them, too.

1. Personal Relationship (Not Denomination Loyalty) is the "New Glue."

Institutional loyalty is much weaker than in the past. The affiliation of people to denominations or specific fellowships, including the affiliation of the churches' leaders to these groups, is also much weaker than it used to be. If the glue of the old is made of values like loyalty, education, and strong belief systems, this is now declining, and the new glue of a strong relational affiliation is strengthening.

Sociologist Robert Withnow from Princeton describes the new reality of the emerging generation in his book, *After the Baby Boomers*.[165] After pointing out how twenty- and thirty-somethings are less inclined to be influenced by the traditional means of institutions, books, magazines, sermons and the like, he draws a pointed conclusion:

> This means that young adults are probably influencing one another in forming opinions about religion much more than they are being shaped by the formal teachings of religious organizations. We are in this sense a culture besieged by information, and yet a society in which so much information has forced us to improvise, to rely on our friends and our personal experiences.[166]

Notice Withnow's words: "influencing one another" and "rely on friends and our personal experiences." He is pointing to a clear trend among younger adults that is also strong among emerging church planters – they are strongly influenced by personal relationships with each other where they share information and common hopes and struggles. On more than one occasion we have seen young church planters express their need for relationships, coaching and mentoring with words like "I am desperate," "I am starving" and "I need these relationships more than you will ever know." This language reflects the needs and the propensity of young leaders to be drawn into networks; especially the relational circles were these needs are often met.

We are not saying that affiliation based upon beliefs, institutional loyalty and past experiences do not matter. But what we are saying is that they matter less now and that young leaders are strongly influenced by the relationships that actively support and equip them in the adventure of church planting.

When given a choice they are less likely to attend conferences, seminars and gatherings unless these gatherings are primarily about personal relationship connections. Conferences are out. Relational hubs are in. It is not just that they value personal connections. Young leaders also do not find special speakers or lectures to be as interesting as their forefathers did – after all, they can download the best sermons and lectures from around the world at the drop of a hat.

2. Networks Foster Participation and Equality in Decision Making.

Networks are decentralized, provide little or no hierarchy, have no headquarters and require decision making by those who are "in the network." In this environment everyone can speak and no one is "the boss." To be sure, healthy networks uphold minimum standards and good church planting practices, but beyond these basics rarely is anyone "in charge." The members of the network circle decide and they also commit and act. They have more ownership of the church planting projects—they are in charge.

Young leaders often want to be accepted in discussions and decision making as equals. The viewpoints of Millennials, when participating in an organization or group as people in their twenties, are just as valuable as anyone else. They struggle to give special respect to position, age, experience and education. They like network environments where everyone has an equal voice to speak and decide. They naturally resist hierarchies. Our culture has trained emerging leaders to believe in themselves and their ideas. They think they should have as much input as anyone else.

Denominations must find ways for younger leaders to speak into church planting plans and strategies. They must be enlisted to help make decisions as equals along with those who are older just as networks do in church planting projects.

3. Young Leaders Typically Support Missions When Personally Connected.

They are more hesitant than their forefathers to give money directly to a denomination or even the local church. They want a personal connection to the cause or the person leading the cause or both before they will truly get behind it. This is true of their resources generally but especially with their financial resources.

Denominations must find ways for younger leaders to "own the vision, strategies, and plans" because it gives them a personal connection with church planting. Without this personal connection, leaders will resist providing financial support. The old adage is especially true with Millennials: *they own what they help create.*

Network structure is ideal for those leaders, especially younger ones who are used to making decisions for themselves and who want to be personally involved when they commit the funds at their disposal. Younger leaders like to have a personal connection to that which they will support (with their resources, financial or otherwise). If you want younger leaders to support church planting or denominational projects, they need to have a say in how the money is spent!

When church leaders decide on the projects that they support and, they tend to have a much higher sense of ownership and support for the church planter. They do not want what they have decided upon and supported to struggle or fail. More and more people have ownership of the mission. The church plant project and the church planter receive much more support than when a mission agency or other denominational leader sends them out.

4. Young Leaders Crave Personal Support, Mentoring and Coaching.

Many of them had no meaningful father figure in their lives and long to be shepherded and to receive guidance from older respected leaders. They want guidance from the foundation of a close personal relationship where mutual respect has been established.

In my (Bobby) experience, most church leaders who are over forty-five do not understand how important it is to develop relationships with younger leaders. Many young men tell me how they long for older men who will just spend time with them, getting to know them, rather than just telling them what to do. Denominational leaders must find ways to personally and relationally invest in and mentor young leaders, as networks do, in ways that are highly relational and personal.

5. Many Younger Leaders Crave "Innovative Ways of Doing Church."

Many young leaders feel great distance between themselves and the established church and they struggle to get excited about a church unless it represents a new, creative or forward- looking structure. They often see the established church structures as no longer effective. It is hard for them to connect with doing church in ways that they think no longer makes sense.

Denominations must find ways to embrace innovation, missional direction and risk-taking faith. Church planting leads the way of effective disciple-making in our day. New churches can start with new structures, new wineskins and new approaches. When this happens, everyone in the network learns. Innovation and improvement for all participating churches increase. Everyone involved can improve the effectiveness of how they do discipleship in their ministries.

6. Younger Leaders are Drawn to the Kingdom of God and Missional-Incarnational Church.

Millennials have been raised with clarity that the Kingdom of God is the reign and rule of God. The Kingdom expresses itself in the church, but the Kingdom is also expressed beyond the walls of any church. Denominations must learn, as many networks have learned, to position the planting of churches within the context of the kingdom of God, not the propagation of a denominational tribe.

The missional-incarnation church is very attractive to young leaders because, in addition to reaching lost people, it focuses upon social justice and the poor. The missional church is still new but we believe it is here to stay, in one form or another, because it seems to capture better than the traditional church, the holistic balance young leaders crave.

Denominations must learn, as the best networks have, to embrace a theology focused on the kingdom of God and more missional models for doing church. In short, denominations must find the flexibility within themselves to plant innovative and new styles of church.

Interview with Ed Stetzer on Networks and Denominations

On Wednesday February 16th, 2011 we interviewed Ed Stetzer to help our readers understand the ways in which denominations can apply the principles of networks.[167] The following question and answer session was taken from that interview:

Question: *Is it a wise move if denominations can become more like networks?*

Stetzer: I think you're talking about denominations becoming more network-like, and I think that makes sense. I think denominations are a lot bigger deal than networks right now. Networks are kind of the sexy thing, but the reality is that the vast majority of church planting is done by denominations, not by networks. Now, in my view, I'm a pro-network-guy and I'm a pro-denomination-guy. For me, I'm a pro-cooperation-guy and both of those are expressions of cooperation. A recent study of the Washington D.C. corridor demonstrates the point: 81 percent of the churches planted were planted by denominations, 11 percent by networks, and then the rest had some connections between the two. So you're talking an 8 to 1 ratio between the two. So I think I'm certainly pro-networks but I am also pro denominations.

Question: *How can denominations become more network-like?*

Stetzer: I think we have to look at what are some of the things that networks have done. Well, first let me say, that denominations can't become networks in some ways, because for example, you know denominations are going to have a generally more defined theological center than networks will have. Now in the case of where you guys are in Stadia—Stadia is a (and you hate the term) but it's an intra-denominational network. You have a confessional identity that drives you and it lines up with the confessional identity of the independent Christian church movement. And so when you do that, you're a network within a family (in your case, it's a non-denominational denomination), but you're a network within a family of churches. So that's not dissimilar—it's just really an extension of the partnerships within denominations.

Question: *Can denominations embrace diversity the way many network embrace it?*

Stetzer: Most denominations have more concerns about secondary and tertiary issues than networks. For example, Acts 29 has what they call an "open-hand" on issues like baptism. Well, I don't know any denomination—well that's not true, there is a couple—but there are no major denominations that have an open-hand on issues like baptism. I mean Baptists like baptism so much; they name their denomination after it. And so they're not going to say, *Hey let's plant churches that baptize infants.* Presbyterians follow a covenantal view of infant baptism. So I think networks tend to have more broad theological persuasions, and thus, if you look at primary issues and secondary issues and tertiary issues, denominations are going agree to disagree on tertiary issues—how you worship, how you dress, what time you meet—that kind of stuff. Whereas networks are more easily going to agree to disagree on secondary issues, like the egalitarian-complimentarian dialogues, whereas denominations tend to agree on both first and second order issues.

Question: *how can denominations act more like networks?*

Stetzer: I think that denominations can be network-like, but they're not going to be as broad as networks. I think that the way they can do that is to create affinity fellowships within their denominational community that are *network-like*. Now, by affinity fellowships, I think that one of the reasons networks work—lets take Stadia— Stadia is largely a connection of contemporary churches within the independent Christian movement that tended to launch large, using teams, and those are all values that undergird the movement (I recognize that there are exceptions to that). Acts 29—primarily younger, indie-rock listening, urban church planters; and GlocalNet tends to be driven by certain values. But they all have certain affinity with one another, but denominations have an affinity generally based on theology. Whereas networks tend to have an affinity based upon methodology or socio-cultural focus or things of that sort. Now there are exceptions, but in networks people end up getting together with people in networks that are like them, doing similar things, and they can relate to well. When denominations get together, you have the guy with jeans with the untucked shirt next to the guy in the suit and tie, next to the Latino pastor who barely speaks English, next to the African-American pastor in a three-piece suit, who are all gathered together because of the same theological affinity. It is harder to build relational bridges in a denomination than it is in the network because the networks tend to look more like. It's easier to be friends with people more like you. Now, that has some negatives, too

Question: *because much of the pull of networks, as you describe, is being with people who are like you, how can denominations embrace this kind of thing?*

Stetzer: First they can recognize that churches are going to network, whether or not the denominations like the idea of networks. Churches are not asking for the denominations permission to form up a network. When a Presbyterian Church of America church is joining Acts 29 network, they're not calling their Presbytery and saying, "hey is this okay with you?" As a matter of a fact, I would guess their Presbytery would rather not, because their presbytery is likely to think, "Hey, you're taking all that energy and you're putting all that energy into Acts 29 when we'd like you to put all your energy into the Presbytery." And so I think that denominations have to first recognize that churches can join networks without the permission of the denomination in almost every denominational setting. Take the appeal of the Association of Related Churches (ARC). They are Pentecostal/Charismatic friendly—which is very attractive to many Pentecostal church planters. Many Assembly of God (AG) leaders will be drawn to a network like that, so they've got to realize in the AG is they will want to be network like, so it would be good to create affinity groups within that denominational family. So for example, if I want to bottle some of the network energy, I need to get my—those who see themselves as missional-incarnational-organic-church-plant-types—I need to get them in a common learning community together. And if I want to make that intra-denominational, within the denomination, it would be good. Within a denomination, I would want an affinity group of Purpose Driven, an affinity group of new reformed, an affinity group of missional-incarnational, and so on.

Question: *how can denominations self-consciously promote networks?*

Stetzer: I would partner with churches that are creating networks. I think that is one of the things that the Presbyterian Church in America (PCA) did well. They got out of the driver's seat of a support role for church planting. They actually got behind their churches while their churches were forming networks. So for example, the Redeemer network (based out of Redeemer Presbyterian Church, in New York, with Tim Keller as lead pastor) is a network that is supported by the infrastructure that denominational leaders have helped to foster and create. And so they work with the denomination in assessment, in coaching, and so forth. The denomination, instead of being afraid of the formation of networks, has actually said that if our churches want to plant this way, we're going to partner with them. Likewise, the Foursquare denomination made similar moves. When they asked me to come and be the coach and consult with them for a while (and I still am), one of things we talked about is how they could become a network of networks. So the denomination has said, "The end goal is not the advance of the denomination but the work of the kingdom as expressed through the local church." And if local churches have determined that the best way they can do that is to form networks, then denomination is wise to create space *and* create resources so they can be a network of networks. Now, there are challenges with that because if you ask the typical pastor, *"where's your loyalty?"* sometimes their loyalty is more to the network than to the denomination but I think if you can work and say that this is a partnership between the two it is good. We want to be part of a bigger *family* of churches, so let's embrace the affinity energy that's there, but at the same time I'm connecting to a large denominational family.

Question: *how can church leaders help in this process?*

Stetzer: I would say is that you want to let local churches lead on this, and again I think you can't create a network because you think it's a "cool idea" and you're a denominational leader. I think you can help churches, and I think churches will be more likely to stay in the family when they're recognized and affirmed as part of the family, even as they're creating some networks along the way. So I think that, once again, it comes back to what I said a minute ago— denominations provide a supporting role—letting local churches lead out. Too many denominations are afraid of the mission strategies of their local churches and networks are one of the missions strategies that is going to grow. I think networks are not going away. I think you're going to see more and more networks forming, but I think what's happening is people are rethinking them.

Question: *what can denominational leaders do?*

Stetzer: I think you need to be willing to rethink denominational structures. I think most denominational structures were created during a time when we rode horses to our meetings and we met once a year and that's the only time we saw each other. I think one of the things you see in networks is they have created communities that were unimaginable and impossible when most denominations were formed. Thus, you often have multiple levels or layers (depending upon their polity) that probably now overlap and are doing the same thing, and if that's the case, you need to ask the hard question, "Are we being a good steward of the resources that the churches give us?" Networks are often providing resources and relationships, which used to be gained from the denomination. Perhaps we can ask, "Is this denominational structure the right structure for the twenty-first century?" When I consult with denominations, I'm always fascinated that they are having the same conversation—they're talking about networks, they're talking about how they are not doing as well as they should. They often feel like their denomination is falling apart—every denomination does—they feel all of those things. So, you know, I would say that it's not an uncommon question—"how do we relate to networks?" The answer has to be, "What are local churches looking to do and how can we reorder our strategy?" And I think too many denominations are too focused on the maintenance of the system, and they need to sometimes re-ask the question, "Is the system accomplishing what we intended it to do?" It may have accomplished that when people rode horses to the meetings. *Does it now accomplish that when people go to meetings online, virtually and actually create communities and share resources together?*

Question: *why do so many denominations feel like they are falling apart?*

Stetzer: You know, I would say that every denomination I work with thinks that it is in some form of a crisis, though the level of the crisis might be different. I was meeting with the leadership of the Foursquare and I said, *How many of you think you're denomination is in a crisis? Raise your hand right now.* And I'd say the strong majority did. I did the same thing with a group of Baptists, *How many? Raise your hands.* It was a strong majority.

I think part of it is that denominations have lost something that really drew them together and it was tribal loyalty. There was historically a tribal loyalty along the way that denominations felt and in the process they were, you know kind of, I mean, if you were Baptist, you went to a Baptist church and you kind of connected with that. Pentecostals would hang with Pentecostals. I think some pastors are post-denominational than people because they think; *I don't want to just be identified with just one denomination.* So I think that denominational loyalty is declining. Part of that is because churches are learning from other churches. A Methodist church might way, "*I don't need the Methodist publishing house for resources. I get them from Purpose Driven.*" I think that, at the end of the day, people are looking to other places on how to do ministry. And, we often are loyal to those from whom we learn. That concerns many denominational leaders.

Question: *are there other reasons for denominational decline and increased interest in networks?*

Stetzer: I think the lack of tribal loyalty is part of it. Increasingly, people don't like to be identified denominationally. People used to say, "I am a Presbyterian." Then a few decades later, "I'm a Christian, first, and a Presbyterian second." Soon it became, "I'm a Christian primarily." So part of it is a cultural issue.

Yet, I do think that a lot of reason you have networks getting traction is because churches feel that it enables them to engage in what God has call them to do at a sharper and more focused level. I think one of the things is that people feel denominations, true or not, have become focused on the wrong things.

People say, "Well, I give to my denomination," and they often see their denominational giving as a tax that they don't know where it goes. So if I give, for example, two percent to the national office, the question is: "*What is it paying for?*" They're not sure. Whereas when they give to the network, they know the people involved, they know the plants that it's sponsoring.

In a network, people perceive that there is: 1) a higher connectivity with where the resources are being spent, and 2) a higher confidence that it's being spent on things that it should be spent on and in the process of spending that their resource dollars are going to where they want them to be.

I think what you find is—and I don't have scientific evidence to back this up—but I think what you'd find is that churches involved at the network level are often involved financially and personally in the activities of that network because they see it as more lined up with their DNA and their values and they tend to see the denomination as more distant and perhaps doing other things than primary things. Now I think that there's a mistake to that process, as well, because ultimately like if there were only a church planting networks, then what about the orphan and the widow? I think if you're only a church-planting network, where are you going to do theological education? Acts 29 didn't have a school, so they forged partnerships with seminaries. Then, they started a school (Re:Train). So, you have to ask, at what point does Acts 29 actually become a denomination? When it creates its own seminary, for example?

Question: *can denominations become focused, as networks are focused, on church planting?*

Stetzer: I think in some ways, *yes*, and in some ways, *no*. I do believe that denominations will be smaller and more focused in the years to come, and I'm not afraid of that. I think right now denominations are in a time of rethinking, and the fastest growing segment as a percentage of Protestant Christianity in America today is non-denominational. So I think you're going to find that denominations are going to think hard about their mission—and I think this is a good thing. It's forcing denominations to think about who they are and what they're doing. And I think they'll be better in the long run because of that process.

Question: is one of the things that is going to scare denominations, as they think about shifting to a network focus, going to be the finances?

Stetzer: Yeah, it's a tough one, because I think one of the things you have to consider. Part of the challenge within a denominational family is that, depending up how you do things; some can direct their giving where they want. See, you all come from the same kind of tradition I do—what we call a low-church, evangelical denomination. You know a lot of evangelical denominations can't do that. So in other words, if you're Lutheran, you're not supposed to give money to other directions. But when you're in a tradition like mine, you know they can give some here and some elsewhere.

If you are a denominational leader, I would say that the case has to be made that giving to the denomination is actually better stewardship. I think the competition will force the denominations to prove that they are the most efficient and effective way to give, and I tend to think that they often are from what I have seen. Now there's always waste in every system and there's always bureaucracy in every system. Of course, one man's system is another man's bureaucracy. So there are always those issues along the way. But, in reality, many denominations do really well with their resources.

I remember a few years ago, my denomination put out a brochure showing what giving to the common mission fund in our denomination supported. They showed that it supported a certain number of seminaries, a certain number of colleges, a certain number of chaplains, missionaries, and so forth. Then they compared that giving to several major para-church ministries using the same amount of money). These were good ministries, but it took a much larger amount to support the para-church ministries to equal the systems and the structures that were in place with our denominational structures.

Question: so you think a lot of the denominational structures should stay intact?

Stetzer: I believe that churches should decide, under the leadership of the Holy Spirit, what is the best way to support God's mission through their church. And if they think a network is to do that, I think a network needs to be the way to do that. In my observation, I've seen denominations to be an effective way to do that. Denominations are getting a lot done, often without notice.

When you go overseas and you go to the last frontier of the ten/forty window you don't often find, *I'm sent out by such and such network*. No... you find PCA missionaries, Assemblies of God missionaries, SBC missionaries, and the like. I'm pro-networks and have spoken to dozens of network meetings, but I think we need to learn to walk and chew gum at the same time and that both networks and denominations need to exist and both need to be valued and both need to be working together for the gospel and the kingdom.

Question: What are some things that networks can do to make themselves friendlier to denominations?

Stetzer: The cooperative and collaborative attitude does need to go both ways. As we have said, there are things that denominations do that networks don't. Networks have to allow people who are in their network to support and be connected to their denominational system and their denominational obligations. I think if I'm a network, I should say, "you need to first give to your denominational connection and support your fair share, and then anything you give above that should go to the network." So I think helping denominations to see that you're not trying to undercut them. I will tell you my experience is that most network churches are also denominational churches and the denomination is often giving more money to the church plant than the network is. Now that's not always the case, but it's very common that it is the case. And so what I would say is that I think you've have to respect that process and that strategy.

Second thing is I'd be very careful not to demean denominations. Denominations are not the dinosaurs of the past. Denominations are very much engaged in mission in the present. And again, that's not cool to some, that's not sexy, but that is statistically accurate. I would say if you're going to be partners, you're going to have to act like partners. That doesn't mean secretly or privately demeaning the partners as well. And that goes both ways, because I hear denominational leaders demeaning networks at times as well.

Question: What do you see for a possible path into the future?

Stetzer: I think it would be a fascinating thing to engage the networks in partnership with the denominational strategy to focus on certain mission projects and endeavors that require a higher level of involvement. For example, let's say there's a network in Houston that forms of contemporary church planters in Houston, that's a part of the Assemblies of God or some other denomination. I would say, I think the wise denomination would invite that network and say to that network, *We're so glad you're there, you're planting churches in and around Houston, but as a network, why don't you adopt this certain people group in Turkey and we have missionaries on the ground there too.*

I think the future involves multiple partnerships. I think the future may look in some ways in churches like NASCAR—where you have kind of a series of logos on your car. I think church planters are very entrepreneurial and very smart and I think you know that they sometimes wear the logos to get the funding—but that's not why you should be in a denomination or a network.

Church planters need to have integrity to only join networks and denominations that they can actually be involved and engaged with along the way. But if they join a denomination and a network—it would be hard to join more than that with integrity—I would encourage them to be involved in both.

For example, most church planting networks are local, not all, but most are going to be U.S.-focused or even regionally focused. And so to be involved with a denomination at the same time gives you some global opportunities as well that aren't there within the network. I think denominations should not see networks as threats but I think networks need to work to be less threatening.

Question: If you had a guy in a room—he's young, wanting to plant a church—what would you tell him to give him to inspire him to work with both a network and a denomination?

Stetzer: I think I would say to him that unless this network is comprehensive, much like more of a denomination is, the network is probably not going to be the only way that this local church is going to connect in God's global mission. But, if that pastor wants to be in both, I would encourage ways to find partnerships in both. But what I would mostly say is to remember that God has called that pastor and that church to be engaged in God's mission globally, and by globally I'm not just talking about internationally, I mean everywhere—here, there, everywhere. If that's the case, if God's called us to be involved globally, then they need to be a steward of the resources that God has given them.

And, would want my people involved at a higher level. I think is that one of the reasons that people are being attracted to networks is that they want a higher level of involvement. If I was pasturing in Cleveland, I'd be open to getting involved in a network there so my people could also be involved.

For me, it boils down to what God is calling that local church to do. Denominations and networks are tools, not the goal. The advance of the gospel is the goal. I think we need to discerningly use those tools to accomplish that scriptural goal.

8

PART ONE: CONCLUSION

In this chapter:
- A summary of Part One
- Further insights on what happens when leaders work together

We have now come to the end of Part One. We have sought to persuade and inform you about the importance, mission and nature of church planting networks. By this point we hope we have both inspired and enlightened you. No doubt you can tell that we are passionate about these things and we hope you will join us.

By way of summarizing the most important principles at work within networks, we thought you would benefit from a series of statements. These statements capture the essence of the principles we have described and encapsulate the key concepts of church planting networks.

1. We all must find ways to support North American church planting.

The truths of the gospel show us that the stakes could not be higher. Jesus' kingdom is the best thing any person can ever experience and we want everyone to have the best opportunity. Christianity is declining here at home and church planting is the best response possible.

2. Networks support church planting at both national (macro) and local (micro) levels.

Church planting requires a high level of personal and relational support and networks are ideally suited to provide it. The networks discussed typically have both a national and a local presence. The network focus, however, is decentralized and focuses on local micro-networks.

3. Apostolic leaders inspire national networks.

We cannot find national or macro networks that do not have apostolic leaders. These are visionary men, strong, bold and full of faith. They are essential for large-scale networks. An apostolic leader typically is joined by a team of other leaders, and together, they inspire and draw followers. Apostolic leaders are the primary vision casters of the movement.

4. Coaches guide local networks.

The real life change in networks typically occurs at a local level. In these face-to-face gatherings, people know each other by name. Network coaches provide support and guidance for the group. These "catalysts" ensure that the members of the group know what to do and they "coach" the members of the network so the members make all the major decisions for themselves.

5. Networks are built around shared DNA.

Apostolic leaders create or synthesize DNA. Then each network is built around that specific DNA. A prime sign of a true apostolic leader is their strong sense that what they believe is right, uniquely right, and life changing - and that it must be propagated. For a network, the DNA becomes the most fundament building block. Relational circles are then built around the DNA and express themselves in the kingdom mission of planting churches.

6. True fellowship (*koinonia*) is at the core of network relationships.

Networks are built around DNA, but they thrive on relationships. Everyone in the network shares life and resources. No one ministers alone. The sharing (which is true *koinonia*) involves the sharing of money, training, personal support, cutting edge resources and general kingdom-life. Without relationships, networks cannot function. By relationships, networks can transform lives, communities, regions and even countries.

7. Networks are transforming the way church leaders associate, plant churches and participate in denominations.

Networks are on the leading edge of effective ministry today, but they will not eliminate denominations. The focus of kingdom life in a network model is the network itself, but there are ways to partner with denominations. Under the careful guidance of wise leaders, a structure to support exiting denominations while multiplying networks and their influence is possible. Alignment with a church or church leaders' DNA must be continuously scrutinized and guarded.

Supporting Leaders Pursuing the Kingdom Mission

Before anything else, networks are about relationships and mission. As we see it, there are numerous benefits in a network collaboration that is focused on relationships and mission.

- Relational support
- Focusing resources on the mission of reaching lost people
- Participation from churches of all sizes
- Shared and expanded vision
- Unity
- Shared resources (especially finances)
- Coaching
- Leadership development
- Encouragement and shared burdens
- Multiplying exponential kingdom-impact

In the introduction, we shared a story of what it's like to plant a church alone. The young leader who planted the church tried his best but had inadequate training, few people and fewer funds. The day that was supposed to be one of the greatest days of his life was disastrous. Only twenty-two people showed up opening Sunday. Even now the church struggles. That should never happen and with networks it doesn't have to happen.

Planting together tells an entirely different story. We want to end this section of the book with hope, with the story of a successful church-planting network. This story is not about a single pastor who pulled up his bootstraps and mustered up the courage to go out there and do it *alone*. This story is about a group of leaders set on church planting who accomplished an amazing feat for the kingdom *together*.

Here is their story: "It's been two and a half years since we planted our last church. Either we've got to get on with this or we've got to dissolve," one of the members said to the network four years ago.[168] They hit a crisis of mission. Terry Martell and this micro-level network in Northeast Wisconsin started meeting ten years ago and their drive was fading. Terry has been a national co-director of LEAD teams for Converge Church Planting. He trains and resources LEAD coaches to catalyze mission around the country. Before he was a national director, he planted two churches and started a LEAD team in his area near Green Bay.

Ten years ago, he and six pastors from his area started the Northeast Wisconsin LEAD team. All the churches are a part of Converge Worldwide and none of them were over two hundred people when they joined together. They all live in small areas, ranging from four hundred to forty thousand in population (except for Terry in Green Bay). They planted churches but over time their focus faded. About this time one of them stood up and said, "Either we've got to get on with this or we've got to dissolve." They decided to get on with it at a 24-hour gathering when the Holy Spirit convicted them to plant more churches.

They were at a rural retreat center, isolated from the world, just the ten of them together for the 24-hour gathering. After they caught up with each other over lunch, they goofed off for a while in the afternoon. (They always have a relational element, Terry says). They came back together for dinner, and then broke off into triads for prayer and accountability. Terry tells the story of what happened next:

> As we were involved in our prayer time for one another, there seemed to be this growing intensity in the groups all around the building—that we can do more, that we need to step up—and it was a God moment. God seemed to be speaking to multiple

groups during our prayer time. Guys were coming up afterwards and saying, "I have to step up on the LEAD team—I either have to plant a church or I have to get my church to significantly support church planting." So we came together the next morning and began sharing stories during our worship time. The guys just said, "We will commit to planting at least one church a year from this moment forward."

This event, which happened just three years ago, sparked a fire in this micro network that has produced a church every year since then.

The result of that has been exciting. We planted with three church planters outside of our region: one launched in twenty ten, one will be launching in just another month or so, and the third one will be launching late in 2011. We have another one of our churches that is partnered with the mother church, and just lost a campus pastor in September of 2010. We have two Hispanic church planters who have just come on in the last year and a half. One of them is already active and has . . . a number of satellite groups that are meeting; and the other one will launch sometime in late 2011. Also, we have another intern who is coming on in 2011. That all began to take shape three years ago—when guys were hanging out together, praying together, sharing their lives together—and God began to move.

This story represents a little bit of what networks are, why they exist and how they function. Terry and the guys in his network took time away from their regular pastoral duties to dream about planting churches together. We know that God desires all men to be saved, but if these men did not know how to respond to his calling, they would not have planted churches in this manner. If they had not come together and decided on a specific vision, they would not have accomplished what they have accomplished. Since their inception ten years ago, Terry says, "We've seen seven churches planted, eight church planters supported and coached, we've given away (just our LEAD team) about $85,000 and are currently supporting and coaching six church planters." That's what it's like to plant churches together.

****

What follows in Part Two is an in-depth description of how the church planting networks in our Stadia system function. Similar to the story we just told, we use our story and the lessons we have learned over the years on how to start and sustain church planting networks.

PART TWO:

STADIA CHURCH PLANTING NETWORKS

9

THE STADIA STORY

In this chapter:
- Stadia's history
- How Stadia became "network-centric"
- Stadia's current leadership and focus

This is not a book about mere church-planting theories. There is a place for that, but that is not what this work is all about. This book is based upon our day-to-day, down-in-the-trenches experiences with Stadia (Stadia).

Along with our colleagues at Stadia, we both have first-hand knowledge of what it takes to start churches. We have planted churches and regularly train church planters, coach church planters and facilitate the development of networks. Stadia's main thing is to plant churches through networks, and we work hard to keep the main thing the main thing. Our long-term goal is to plant 100 churches a year through networks.

Stadia was founded in 2003. Our fellowship of churches or Protestant tribe, as some of us like to say, is the Christian Churches/Churches of Christ. We are part of the Restoration Movement which goes back to the first decade of the 1800s in North America and ultimately has its roots in the larger Baptist and Presbyterian movements which originate in the Reformation. In our idealized selves, we like to think that we identify with the original New Testament practices in regard to church structure found in the

Bible and reflected in the early church; hence our broader name, "the Restoration Movement."

Our denominational friends often refer to us as the "non-denominational denomination." We are a fellowship of autonomous churches in relationship with each other because of common mission, beliefs, publications, conferences and gatherings. Our focal gathering is the North American Christian Convention which has been held in the summer of every year since 1924. We are a movement of churches around the world with approximately 5500 congregations in the US and another 5500 churches internationally. For evangelistic purposes, our movement's early leaders in the 1800s often established evangelistic associations, para-church entities which are supported by the free will offerings of our autonomous churches.

The Northern California Evangelistic Association (NCEA) was one of the modern para-church entities in our fellowship of churches in North America. The NCEA focused on evangelistic and church planting endeavors in Northern California.

The NCEA was expanded into a national church planting organization in 2003 and took on the name Stadia. "Stadia" is the word used to describe the dimensions of heaven in Revelation 16:7-- *"The city was laid out like a square, as long as it was wide. He measured the city with the rod and found it to be 12,000 stadia in length, and as wide and high as it is long."* For us the name "Stadia" represents our partnership in God's kingdom dream to fill heaven with people by the thousands.

The Northern California Evangelistic Association and Our DNA

The roots of Stadia are strongly tied to the NCEA and Dean Pense. The NCEA began a new era of effectiveness when Dean became the leader in 1986. By the time Stadia's current president, Marcus Bigelow, took over the leadership of NCEA beginning in 1998, that period of effectiveness had imprinted itself firmly on the organization. So, before we tell the story of Stadia, we want to acknowledge four of the more important elements of our organization which trace themselves back to Dean Pense and his leadership during the NCEA days.

Dean's first step was bold and risk-taking faith. When Dean assumed the leadership of NCEA, in 1986, he took over an organization that in the prior thirty-two years had witnessed the planting of only sixteen churches. Dean cast a vision to plant forty-five churches by 2000. That vision and Dean's stubborn will to walk closely with God and see it come to fruition–made all the difference in the world. It actually took until 2002 for those forty-five churches to be planted, but NCEA experienced unparalleled growth and success because of Dean's faith and leadership. Now it is just a part of the way we approach things on a daily basis. It displays bold, risk-taking faith every time a network is initiated and a church is planted.

Second, Dean focused on the willing people and was not deterred by the unwilling. He was not afraid of opposition. When he arrived to lead NCEA, not everyone was in favor of increased church planting and many were skeptical of the ability to plant churches at all. Dean experienced many frustrations and roadblocks, but his faith was undaunted. He decided to entrust himself to God and not be overly concerned about those who could not see or believe the vision.

To help with his own frustration, he coined a phrase we still use today--"Go with the Goers." His focus on supportive, positive leaders has paid eternal dividends. NCEA planted with whoever was willing to come on the journey and would not allow naysayers to thwart the fact they were doing big things for God.

Third, Dean embedded in the DNA of NCEA (and now Stadia) an intimate care and concern for church planters. Church planting is not for the faint of heart. The leadership challenges, disappointments, struggles and slow victories often necessitated special support. Dean initiated planter care "huddles." Church planting leaders were enlisted to help and support one another.

The priority of relationships was firmly established during the Dean Pense era. The care and relational support for church planters was not so much a matter of institutional organization as it was an organic commitment to provide whatever personal help church planters needed. It often began with two or three planters in a booth at a restaurant like Denny's and gradually it was built into a full planter care system. As more churches were established, huddles focused on authenticity and transparency, praying for and encouraging one another.

Fourth, Dean established a financial model that propelled and sustained reproducing church planting. In the late 1980s Dean knew that the model of financially supporting church planting which was being practiced would not work. Something had to change. He described to me (Bobby) a night of wrestling with God in prayer over the need to plant churches but with the barrier presented for the vision by the lack of funding. He wrestled all night with God, asking for a breakthrough. Then he gained clarity. Dean described it this way: "After wrestling with the Lord, I finally gave in."

Dean committed to God that he would ask each planter to give back 10 percent of the church's income to church planting. The first planter Dean called upon to make this commitment resisted, but Dean was not deterred. From that night and to this day, every Stadia planter commits to giving back 10 percent of regular tithes and offerings to church planting. This commitment now witnesses a healthy flexibility--typically 5 percent goes to support Stadia's church planting efforts and another 5 percent goes to the church planting network projects that are individually chosen by the church planter.

We all stand on the shoulders of those who have gone before us. Dean Pense bequeathed to Stadia a legacy that positions us for great things in the future. We give our thanks to him.

NCEA and Marcus Bigelow

As a church planter, I (Marcus) was supported by Dean Pense and the NCEA. After years of leading the church I planted, I was asked to take on the leadership mantle of Stadia in 1998. I received a solid foundation from Dean and sought to continue and expand our church planting activities.

In 1998 I attended a conference led by Dr. Bob Logan and Dr. Steve Ogne. In their teaching on being a "New Church Incubator" they suggested that any organization wanting to make a difference would assess church planters and train them as well as support them emotionally and spiritually. At the time I felt like we could barely spell assessment, but I came home and initiated both assessment and a bootcamp. With the huddles already initiated by

Dean Pense, this triad of planter care, assessment, and bootcamps became the foundations for the future.

Our first attempts with assessment and bootcamp were just that—attempts. But we refined, improved and expanded them so they became quality processes. It cannot be understated how Phil Claycomb and Roger Gibson made all the difference in these efforts. They became part of the team and brought their significant expertise to assessment and boot camp.

There has always been a NCEA/Stadia bias to adopt a good idea and get started instead of waiting to perfect it. This bias to action first--to risk-taking faith and innovation--has allowed us to try new things and has also translated into a "can do" attitude among our church planters. Innovate and improve, innovate and improve again has been our *modus operandi*.

Another bias of NCEA and then Stadia is generosity. We believe it is important to bless others with the blessings we have received. We freely gave away the ideas that were working for the good of the Kingdom. At least four other organizations have developed assessments, bootcamps and coaching systems after going through the process with Stadia. We are grateful for this opportunity. As we like to say, "The copyright, after all, belongs to the King, and we are about Kingdom business."

We were also regularly asked to help other evangelistic associations and organizations. Then in 2002 plans were laid to expand outside of Northern California. By early 2003 we had transitioned from NCEA to Stadia.

Provision Ministry Group, Church Development Fund and Stadia

The Provision Ministry Group is an umbrella organization which coordinates a family of five ministries serving Christian Churches/Churches of Christ in North America. Provision was established in 2003 to provide direction, leadership and support services to a growing family of "ministry partners." Church Development Fund (CDF,), Visioneering (an organization that develops design and building plans), and Stadia were the first three. In the past 6 months, Kairos Legacy Partners and the Co-mission Fund have also been birthed in the Provision family.

In our fellowship, Church Development Fund (CDF) has served since 1953 as a non-profit funding organization to help churches and Christian organizations finance and build churches. CDF serves as a Christian supported bank--without profits for individuals--which exists for the purpose of helping churches and Christian organizations build the structures they need. CDF has enabled countless churches to build that would never have been built at least not as inexpensively as with CDF.

Since CDF successfully developed a pool of resources for ministry, it was decided that some of these resources could be used to help church-planting. Since 2003 CDF has given millions of dollars to Stadia for church planting. Stadia is blessed to have such a close relationship with a Kingdom-minded organization that focuses on church planting.

Within just a few months a number of other regional church-planting associations among Christian Churches/Churches of Christ joined Stadia to provide rapid national expansion mostly across the Sunbelt region of the U.S. (Southern California, Arizona, Georgia, Louisiana, and Southeastern Texas). By late 2003, Stadia expanded into many of these states. It was at this time that I (Bobby) joined the Stadia's leadership along with Greg Marksberry and several other leaders including Dr. Tom Jones. Tom's leadership was very dynamic from the first days of 2003 as he helped establish and expand Stadia into the Eastern United States. More recently Tom began serving as Stadia's National Executive Director.

Stadia From 2003 to 2005

From 2003 to 2005, Stadia expanded rapidly--too rapidly to be sustained. We planted many churches and established many effective processes. Among the effective processes established or enhanced were planter care systems, better coach systems and utilization, along with bootcamps for training and online tools. Todd Wilson, with Exponential Network, helped Stadia identify and expand our ability to help church planters, especially with the online project management system they designed for church planters. But, like other organizations that expand too fast, Stadia faced a crisis. We did not have a good handle on the scope and financial commitment necessary to sustain our development. Something had to be done.

Our re-evaluation was not just based upon organizational, financial and structural issues. We also came to a realization that historically and philosophically those from our spiritual heritage value decentralization over centralization. Christian Churches/ Churches of Christ do not value hierarchy, institutionalism and centralizing movements. Although we do not want to be a formal denomination, without realizing it, Stadia was taking on some of these trappings. We picked the planters, funded, trained and coached them. We then asked them to help us expand. We had become and were perceived as an organization that was "Stadia-centric."

In the fall of 2005, under the guidance of Provision's Larry Winger, along with the help of Todd Wilson, Paul Williams, Tom Jones, Bobby Harrington and others, Stadia self-consciously made major adjustments. The biggest was a switch to the decentralized network model described in this book. The model which emerged focused on developing networks of church-planting partners, primarily church-planting churches and others who form networks to plant churches in their region.

The major lesson learned by Stadia between 2003 and 2005, is that centralized infrastructure is very expensive and un-scalable. Collaboration is more effective, less costly and scalable. As a result of the switch to the decentralized model, coaching, assessment, bookkeeping and training were outsourced to various providers (in late 2010, training was brought back in-house).

Prior to decentralization, the "one stop shop" model of "send us your planters and your money and we will plant the churches" was a central theme. Since 2005, Stadia's motto has become "we help churches plant churches." The focus has shifted to assisting networks. This has resulted in increased ownership among our church planting partners and networks.

Stadia from 2006 to Early 2011

After our reorganization in late 2005, I (Bobby) was asked to shift my Stadia focus from training church planters and coaches to developing Stadia's networks. My previous work with training church planters and coaches was transferred to Church Coaching Solutions, a new organization Todd Wilson (Exponential) and I created, along with two other colleagues, to train coaches and church planters from all types of Evangelical churches. I spent a lot of time talking to Marc Bigelow, Tom Jones, Todd Wilson and Dean Pense. Even though he was retired from Stadia leadership, Dean Pense had spent a lot of time up until 2005 developing networks in California. His leadership instincts were sharp--it seemed that everything I learned in books, conversations and from other networks, he had been developing. He simply sensed that it was the best future for church planting.

The network process we describe in the next chapter pulls together our best insights as a Stadia team. The leadership strength of our team, under Tom Jones' executive leadership, is in the synergy of our experience in church planting. We have learned from leaders like John Wasem who has focused on management teams and coaching (with over 25 years of experience in church planting) to Debbie Jones with insights about the needs of spouses (a church planter's wife who ministers to the wives of planters), to Roger Gibson's seasoned insights about people (both very wise and very young in his mid 70s), to Brent Foulke's insights about assessment, leadership, coaching and networks, to David Limerio with his compassion for the struggles of church planters, to Dan Converse who has focused on finances and helped create financial systems for non-detailed church planters (along with others too numerous to mention). God has blessed us with a model and a system, which provides tremendous support for both networks of churches and for church planters.

Prior to the network model being adopted, Stadia had an 83 percent success rate. Since adopting the network model five years ago Stadia now are success rate that is well above 90%. The power and synergy of the network model seems to be obvious. Today Stadia focuses on network formation and planter care.

Based upon early experiences, we have concluded that planters do not need to have vision imparted to them--they already have a God-given vision. Instead Stadia has always viewed its role as protecting, encouraging and supporting the planting family so that their vision could bear fruit. We view our role as drawing out the vision of the planter and the network.

Planter care is costly in both financial and emotional resources. Someone with both the heart and training to come alongside church planters and their families must be empowered to care. In some networks this is done by volunteers, in others it is done by men and women who do it full time. A balance of volunteers and paid professionals is probably the most effective.

Through a rigorous process of strategic planning in 2010, Stadia developed a new structure. Marcus continues as president and Tom Jones serves as executive director. Stadia now maintains two operational teams--a Mobilization Team which concerns itself with helping new networks develop and with recruiting and assessing planters, and a Planter Care Team which assists networks in providing the best planter care possible to their planting teams.

The Mobilization Team is composed of an Associate Executive Director for Mobilization, Brent Foulke, and four regional associate network directors (all part time). These network directors are responsible for recruiting and serving networks in their regions. Each associate network director also assists network coaches in their region. These network coaches lead one or two networks as independent contractors while maintaining full-time ministries.

The Planter Care Team is led by the Associate Executive Director for Planter Care, David Limiero. He is assisted by several specialists that serve planters. These specialists direct the following areas: Project Management, Training, Management Teams and Coaching, and Spousal and Family Care. The Planter Care Team also oversees the outsourced contractors who come alongside the new churches. Many of these outsourced services are listed in the following paragraphs.

Seven Best Practices

We are regularly told that Stadia is at the top of the list in providing networks and systems for church planters. To assist networks planting churches, Stadia has adopted seven "best practices" (none of which are unique to Stadia, though we do have a comprehensive planter and network care package) which it brings to the table in all church plants and networks in which it participates:

1) rigorous assessment of the church planting couple;
2) formation of a management team selected from the network partners with an accountable management team chair;
3) training of the church-planting team in a Stadia-led bootcamp;

4) the employment of a professionally trained church-planting coach for every church plant;

5) a project management system with a project manager to help keep the planters on track;

6) "Bloom!" a care system for lead planter spouses; and

7) professional church-planting accounting for the first two years so that the church plant gets off to a good start.

These seven best practices help us provide the best possible chance for success, and though they are expensive, in the long scheme of things we are sure they are worth it. The cost of a failed plant both financially and spiritually (to the planter and his family and to the community) drives us to provide high-quality care. Stadia is passionate about our expressed goal to provide the highest level of care possible for planters and their families.

Additionally, each network has a network coach to assist, educate and encourage the members. Our experience has shown that planting a church is energy-consuming. Without a coach to help the network build and keep momentum, it is easier for a network to lose energy or get sidetracked by mission drift.

Stadia's Ongoing Vision

As much as we are tempted to look back to celebrate God's work, we dare not do that. Our value of "Holy Discontent" will not allow us to stand still. There is too much to be done in a world that desperately needs transformation. Our ongoing long-term mission and short-term vision is reflected below.

Stadia Brings People and Churches Together to Transform Lives and Communities Through Church Planting.

- Together with our NETWORKS, we plant new churches that have the greatest potential for sustainability by sharing resources, best-practices and support.
- Together with our PLANTERS, we create the healthiest church-planting environment possible by providing the best planter and spousal care, coaching and project management.
- Together with our DONORS, we invest in life transformation by funding new churches with adequate resources to transform their communities.

Our highest priority is to strengthen relationships with and between our NETWORKS, DONORS and PLANTERS. We will do this by investing time in each other, communicating well, delivering on promises and sharing the best each person has to offer (making that expertise readily and easily available).

Stadia's vision is to see thousands of churches planted *transforming millions of lives and thousands of communities* both in the US and around the world. Stadia recently adopted a "glocal" focus for networks. Each network that is forming a US church is also encouraged to plant an international church. Rather than starting from scratch, we would rather form strategic partnerships all over the world to bring about transformation.

One example of this partnership is with Compassion International. In 2011, Stadia networks will partner with Compassion to plant four new churches near Manta, Ecuador. We have identified an indigenous church-planting movement as a partner. Compassion International will place their child advocacy programs in each church, and our new churches in the U.S. will be able to sponsor children in the new churches in Ecuador. This model can be replicated all over the world with many different organizations.

The Power of Networks

The biggest power in networks is the power of collaboration which leads to more churches focusing on church planting, more church plants and better planter care. Additionally, some of the blessings we have seen as a result of networks have been in unity among congregations.

We find biblical examples of congregations collaborating for benevolence in mission in the book of Acts. One of the participants in Stadia's networks recently spoke about the churches with whom they collaborated, "We have really never worked together and planting a church together has unified us like nothing else." This group of churches feels a huge call to mission and collaboration and cooperation. A common mission has been the draw to collaboration and cooperation.

We experience practical unity and autonomy at the same time. Collaboration and autonomy can sometimes be viewed as opposites but in Stadia's experience, voluntary collaboration leads to increased effectiveness, a greater sense of mission and belonging to the Kingdom of God universal rather than just to a single congregation.

Interdependence as a value brings many rewards. One of Stadia's core values is "It's all about relationships." We like to focus on the benefits of working together--we help each other and accomplish more than we could ever do separately. Practically speaking, working together means building trust, taking time to foster relationships and committing to each other in those relationships with energy and shared resources.

We also collaborate with other church-planting organizations and denominational tribes. All of these groups have greatly helped us. For example, as we will describe, Stadia adopted a 24 hour retreat format (fully outlined in a later chapter) that is a key in building these relationships because of the help provided by Converge's Tom Nebel and Gary Rohrmayer.

One final note on network values--Stadia has always valued raising up leaders. This is seen in the number of planters who emerge from earlier plants, from Stadia personnel who have risen into leadership with the organization and with leaders who have gone on to lead other organizations.

10

STADIA'S NETWORK PROCESS

In this chapter:
- Steps for planting a church through church planting networks
- The decisions necessary to plant a church for you and your network partners
- Stadia's minimum standards that produce a high rate of success

At Stadia we see ourselves as a network of local micro networks. Stated differently, we are a network of church planting networks. Each of our local or micro networks has different traits and values, but they are all part of our system. As we are writing this book, we have these networks in twenty-two states.

As the last chapter described, our model is based upon systems that have been proven over time to produce both health in church planters (and their plants) and health in our networks. The diagram below is a picture of our process. The fourteen steps are typical steps, but they are not always uniformly practiced. We learned a long time ago that flexibility is a must in church planting and church-planting networks.

The process as we outline it also assumes that a group of church leaders and churches have come together with an interest in church planting. Recruiting the group is an entirely different process. In the next two chapters we will explain how network coaches recruit churches to the gatherings in which leaders of churches are "coached through this process." We believe that the leaders need to be "coached" so that they make the decisions, own the process and own the church-planting project and the care and support of the church-planting team. In a network it is all about doing church planting "together".

We hope that this introduction to our process helps the reader grasp the various elements of planting a church through a network. We also think it is helpful to see an overview of the process as a whole. I (Bobby) developed this process initially through trial and error and then we developed a consistent rhythm with it.

It is important to note that the process is fluid and sometimes it does not follow the exact path laid out below. It is especially important to note that this process will be modified if a planter adopts a missional or the relational discipleship model (discussed in more detail in the next chapter). These two models, and others, put less focus on a "launch date" or "start date" because they focus, from the first day, on building small, informal gatherings of people as the focus of the church. The church starts the day the planter starts his first small group.

It will make more sense if the reader can look at the process as a whole. Here are the steps:

1. Cast the vision
2. Clarify the covenant and commitments needed
3. Make the covenant (memorandum of understanding)
4. Set up a management team
5. Get the network churches praying
6. Determine the exact place to plant
7. Search for and find a lead planter
8. Uphold Stadia's minimum standards
9. The planter moves into the community
10. The planter casts the vision in network churches
11. The planter builds a launch team
12. The church starts
13. The planter receives ongoing coaching and support
14. We do it again!

Step 1—Cast the vision

Everything starts with vision. The heart of a network is the vision to plant churches. Sometimes this comes from Stadia and at other times it comes from a local church leader. Sometimes a business person or member of a congregation starts the process. Sometimes a vision may come from a church planter who hears of a network and approaches the network for help. In recent years, we have seen the vision emerge from a staff member in a new church who wants to do it again.

The vision may start at step 14 in the network process. It is our belief and experience that when churches are planted successfully, new planters and new vision will emerge out of that church. When this happens it greatly simplifies the process of finding planters for the network in their second and succeeding plants.

Step 2—Clarify the covenant and commitments needed

It is important to clarify what it will take to actually plant a church once a vision has been articulated. This usually involves at least two meetings: one to cast the vision and one to clarify the commitments with time in between for leaders to share the vision with other churches.

When a group of leaders forms a network, there are several unspoken issues being negotiated. First, there is the natural jostling for position that occurs with any group of people. Second, no group begins with a focused agenda. This harmony is achieved only after the give-and-take of several meetings. Third, during the early meetings each group will gauge its relative commitment to the mission. You quickly discover who wants to be on the team and who showed up for free coffee.

As we pointed out in the last chapter, Dean Pense, an early church-planting pioneer for the NCEA, often said "Go with the Goers." If you wait for everyone to commit, you will never begin the project, so you "go" with those who are willing to get on board early. The challenge is welcoming those early adopters while preserving relationships with those who may come along later.

At this phase it is important to count the cost. It is exciting to think about places where the church could be planted, but not so thrilling to figure out how you're going to pay for it. During the clarification phase, figuring out who can and will come to the table with dollars is vital. It always costs money to start a church, and sometimes it is paid by a single mother church, sometimes it is paid by network partners and sometimes it is paid by a church-planting couple who are bi-vocational.

Leaders often do not realize that in a bi-vocational plant, the primary donor is the church planter since the single largest expense in most church plants is planter salary. In our experience it costs about $200,000 of partner money to start a church that can be expected to get above 150 in attendance. Todd Wilson, Director of the Exponential Church Planting Conference tells us that he has found that it costs about $1000 per attendee after two years. Here is what he means: in a suburban environment, it typically costs about $1000 per person up through two to three months after the typical church is launched (i.e., take the average weekly attendance two to three months after launch and you will likely have spent $1000 x # of people attending to get to that point). So, if a suburban church with a strong Sunday morning program hopes to draw around 200 people, it will typically cost around $200,000. Wilson has found it noteworthy to see how consistent this figure is in all kinds of suburban contexts. We have also found this number to be fairly accurate, so we use it for the typical model.

It is important to also clarify, as noted above, that Stadia does not have one type of church that we plant. Our current dominant model (spring 2011) is a combination of both an attraction and missional plant. It is a church which tries to balance Sunday gatherings with a missional focus on serving the community. As we describe it in the next chapter, Stadia has started at least six types of churches in the last several years.

Besides the financial participation issues, the location of the plant is an important issue to be worked through at this point. In a local network this decision can affect one or more of the partners. Most churches are leery of planting a church in their own backyard. This is probably more an issue of perception than reality but nevertheless must be addressed. In a distant partnership getting everyone excited about a location can be a challenge.

Step 3—Make a covenant (a memorandum of understanding)

When your team has emerged you can develop the group covenant. It can take up to eighteen months for a new network to reach this stage. When people are pressured to sign a covenant prematurely, there is often an unacceptably high drop-out rate. This covenant--often called a memorandum of understanding--should be in writing (see examples in the Appendix in the back).

These covenants should include the following commitments:
- A commitment that representatives will come to the meetings with the support and authority of his church.
- Representatives can make decisions, commit funds and help choose the planter without having to ask a board or eldership about each decision.
- Specific expectations regarding the role of each participating church--the amount of funds committed, the timing of those funds, the level of involvement of the leadership and membership.
- The specific nature or model of the church to be planted.

A good covenant should also outline whether a church will send members permanently or temporarily and will let the planter know what type of recruiting will be allowed from each member congregation.

It is important for every leader to sign this covenant. Just as "good fences make good neighbors," good covenants make good partnerships. The signed contract memorializes the work done to this point and it calls for a celebration! Be sure to take a picture of the group and send a copy to each member as a reminder of their commitment.

It is also important for leaders to share the picture and/or commitment which they have made to the network with their church families. Healthy churches make sure that their members know and celebrate their commitment to expanding God's kingdom through church planting. It helps the whole church to embrace this "Kingdom DNA."

Step 4 –Set up a management team

Management teams are set in place to provide care and oversight for the lead church planter. Most networks have some kind of a management team to oversee big picture issues and provide a sounding board for the church planter. Most of the major network partners who are contributing significant dollars to the plant will have a seat on the management team; however, if there are many partners, a management team is often limited to five or less.

While everyone in the network would like to be on the management team, it is not practical. In some networks the number of partners is too many for ongoing decision-making. There are times when a network partner may have too many other commitments to participate on the management team.

We recruit, train and guide a management team chairman from the network partners. He guides the team in their duties since many do not have experience in church planting. The chairman of the team should be knowledgeable not only about church planting but also about church growth in general and good leadership and administration practices. A management team that helps the planter develop good policies early on is a great benefit to the young church. This team should stay out of day-to-day operations. Instead, compare this group to a set of bylaws which is primarily for situations you hope will never happen.

Most networks can name a time when a planter went through a crisis and the management team saved the plant. In some cases the planter was helped and restored. In other cases the planter was removed and the management team helped to find new leadership. It is important for a management team to have good guidelines for operating and the chairperson is responsible to see that the team abides by its charter and commitment.

Management teams run two risks: 1) becoming too operational and "getting in the weeds" or 2) the opposite of becoming such an uninformed rubber stamp that there is no accountability or assistance when needed. The management team is the keeper of the covenant, the MOU. This document outlines the relationships of accountability, responsibility and authority for all involved in the church plant.

The management team must speak with one voice and must not allow individual members to freelance as consultants in the church plant. The management team is also the keeper of the Church Planter Expectation Document (an example of this document is in the appendices). This is a document which clarifies the commitments that are being made by the church planter. It also establishes an accountability role for the management team with the planter.

The balance between authority, accountability and responsibility must be maintained if all connected with the plant are to remain involved and fulfilled with frustrations minimized. If good fences make for good neighbors, then good agreements make for good working relationships in a church plant.

The chairman of the management team must be authorized to negotiate and sign documents on behalf of the team and be the most frequent interface with the planter and other organizations. As you can surmise, the chair should be someone who understands the process and is trusted by all the management team (MT) members. Stadia finds it is helpful to offer the MT chair a small stipend in order to ensure reports to all group members and because it does take a substantial amount of time to fulfill the duties. (See the MT Chair job description and responsibilities document in the appendices.)

Step 5– Get the network churches praying

Prayer is a vital part of healthy church planting. We like to quote Psalm 127:1 and apply it to the church plant project: "Unless the LORD builds the house, its builders labor in vain." Hopefully, leaders within the network have already been praying. Now it is time to take prayer to a wider circle. In the covenant each member church should commit to serious prayer for the new plant. Early topics include praying for a planter, for unity, for the lost and for a specific location for the church. Many networks hold joint prayer meetings.

One of the most effective methods is "praying through an area." In Salt Lake City one network has gathered for the past two years on top of a hill overlooking the city. From this vantage point— which the team has dubbed "Moses Hill"— those who pray can see 20 miles in every direction. As twilight falls and street lights come on, it is easy to understand the magnitude of reaching those who live below. Other groups drive through large areas asking God for wisdom and asking the Holy Spirit to begin drawing people to the new church.

Summit Christian Church in Sparks, Nevada began after months of prayer, walking every street in the city, often through freezing cold. A small team prayed, "God, may your peace be upon this home," in front of *every* house. Pastor Steve Bond believes this to be one reason Summit has become a healthy, growing church. It is significant that this church came from a hill-top prayer meeting overlooking the Reno basin.

Step 6— Determine the exact place to plant

The location of the new plant will determine the type of planter needed. Obviously an upscale, re-gentrifying city neighborhood filled with 20-somethings and a Sun City retirement village require two different kinds of leaders. A careful study of demographics, both formal studies and "shoe leather" observations, are important. Although network members may have impressions of an area based on past experiences or "common knowledge," these impressions are often inaccurate. It is important not to shortcut the process of thoroughly studying a potential area.

After identifying one or more suitable locations, the network members should agree on a general location for the plant. A decision on the specific location within a city or neighborhood is best left to the planter and his management team.

Step 7— Search for and find a lead planter

The most significant predictor of a successful church plant is the leadership of the lead planter. The most important thing a management team can do is to find the right person to lead the church, so the management team must first determine the lead planter profile. Since a planter ministers most effectively to an age group within ten years of his own age, this demographic information allows the network to begin the planter selection process.

Dr. Charles Ridley developed a list of thirteen key characteristics of a church planter which is widely used by many networks. The location chosen will add specific color to this profile. The network should review these qualities and determine its non-negotiables.

More recently, MissionInsite in cooperation with Tom Bandy, has developed a ministry area profile for most regions of the country. Based upon the top population segments represented in the target area, it makes recommendations about what types of minister profile and ministry activities will most likely be successful. While these are generalizations, they are helpful in making some determinations as to planter personality profile.[169]

Several years ago a young couple came with a desire to minister in San Francisco. Having been raised in extremely rural, outdoors-oriented communities, they had absolutely no idea about what living in the city would mean. With some guidance they reconsidered and prayerfully started a church in a community that was more like them. This church soon became the second largest church in town because the planter knew how to relate to the people of the area. This kind of insight is very helpful for management teams to consider as they seek to find a church planter.

Once the profile is established, the network is ready to hire a church planter—the most crucial decision a network will make, one that calls for significant prayer. With the right planter, money and workers and new church members will follow. With the wrong planter, hundreds of thousands of dollars may be spent and dozens of workers discouraged without anyone coming to know Christ.

Good planters come from a number of sources, including successful student ministries, entrepreneurial careers and associate positions in churches. The leader you want is likely not looking for a new ministry. He will have to be recruited to a vision. The majority of church planters do not need to have a vision implanted in them because God has been preparing them. Sometimes however, they need to receive permission from the management team to "go for it".

One of the values of the network is the multiplicity of relationships from which to find the planter. Many times the planter will emerge from within one of the network churches. In our experience many times a youth minister or associate who suddenly becomes impatient in his present position is often in the process of being called.

Forty years ago when church planting was an uncommon event the only options for an emerging leader who needed to try out his leadership was to move on to another church, sometimes with bad feelings left behind. In the worst cases it may cause a split or he could end up getting fired. Now, however, a church can recognize that a young leader needs to be given a chance to "try his wings" and send him out to plant a church with their blessing and encouragement.

No matter the source from which the planter emerges, there is a process that should be followed. First, the management team should interview a potential planter to see if there's chemistry. There are numerous pre-assessment resources that can be helpful to a network before investing the $2500 to $3500 it costs for a full assessment.

- http://www.churchplanting4me.com/tutorial/preassessment.html

- http://www.churchplanterprofiles.com/cake/
- http://www.elichurchplanting.com/

Once results from one or more of these resources are obtained and shared with the management team and network coach, a better decision can be made.

If the results are still positive and all parties want to go forward, a full assessment should be undertaken. There are numerous assessment centers. Stadia uses two such centers:

- Church Planting Assessment Center (CPAC)
  http://www.churchplanting4me.org/
- Discovery Labs
  http://www.discoverylabs.org/id5.html

It is important for the network to remember that no matter who the candidate may be, no matter how well-known or successful, every planter must pass formal assessment before being offered the job. Prior success in a church plant does not guarantee success in the next plant. Only an assessment can tell whether family ties have been broken, whether there is a fit with the potential plant location or whether some other issue has surfaced.

If the planter is well-known to all of the network people, it is tempting to skip this process. We have three words for you--don't do it!! It is an act of love to send a planter through assessment. First, if there is something that will shoot him down, it will save him and his family grief later. As some say about marriage: "The best time to get divorced is before you get married." Second, if a team of twelve or thirteen experienced practitioners of church planting give their approval and encouragement, then the planter is bolstered in his courage to plant.

Third, most often, even when a church planter passes assessment, there will be some areas of coaching needs revealed. This becomes extremely important for the coaching relationship at a further date. Of all the things that a network and management team will do, choosing the right planter is the most important. Assessment is crucial for that.

Step 8— Uphold Stadia's minimum standards

This is where Stadia really helps networks. We ensure that the best practices in contemporary church planting are upheld. We have learned that each of the following processes are essential to the health of the church planting project itself. We call them our minimum standards:

- Assessment of church planting leaders
- Training in a church planter bootcamp
- Personal coaching (by an experienced church planter)
- Project management (hands on guidance through the 100s of small steps in a church plant)
- Accounting services (accounting processes designed for church planters)
- Spousal Care (Bloom)

After hiring a planter, the management team should ensure that he receives current training. Starting in the fall of 2010, Stadia now has our own church-planting bootcamp, but there are other quality training events including Real Life Ministries' bootcamp, Phil Claycomb's Art of the Start and the bootcamp provided by the Church Multiplication Training Center.

It is best for the planter to begin training before moving to his new location. Stadia requires that not only the planter, but also the spouse and when possible, team members attend the training so that everyone is on the same page from the outset.

The coach should be selected at the same time and, if possible, should attend training with the planter. This will give them a shared experience and shared reference points. To ensure quality coaching, Stadia selects the church-planter coach, usually in dialogue with the planter. In this way we ensure that the coach is trained and competent for the task of helping the planter. The coach also provides regular updates to the management team and Stadia leadership because he is often the first one to identify problems. All problems, however, are to be resolved by the management team. The management team, representing the network, is responsible for the plant, not Stadia.

During this early phase it is also important to connect the

planter with whatever resources the network can provide in project management, spousal support, mentoring and peer networks.
Stadia provides a project management coaching tool called Converge, and Bloom, a support network for spouses of men in church planting.

If the planter is attending a bootcamp sponsored by a third party, it is very important for the coach or management team chair or both to attend with the planter so that processes or practical matters are discussed in the formation process. We believe that a planter must come out of bootcamp with a strategic plant plan on paper. This allows the planter to hit the ground running. Moving to a new community without any infrastructure or a clear plan would be almost overwhelming. The bootcamp gives direction to the planter especially in the early going.

Step 9— The planter moves into the community

In a typical setting, the planter moves to the location six to nine months before the church's public launch. This assumes a traditional church plant model, where the church is launched with a large Sunday gathering. We want to plant churches that ministers holistically as an expression of the kingdom of God. At the same time, most of our plants launch with some form of weekly public gathering.

After helping create and develop our network system, I (Bobby) was asked about a year ago to turn my focus to research, development and missional leadership. What this means is that I have been asked to develop an expertise in understanding missional church-planting. Currently Stadia has about fourteen church plant projects under this umbrella. I am learning that there is a lot of energy from young leaders for a purely missional church – focused on those who are poor, on the margins or in an unreached segment of the population.

But there is a problem! These are people who are hard to reach, they take a tremendous amount of time and the growth of the church is slow, often faced with financial challenges. Furthermore it is common for missional planters to be so focused on serving and developing credibility that they burn out. We have learned, at this point, that the planter must first create Christian community (healthy small groups), just like Jesus did and then minister to the lost out of that community. Stadia is committed to learning about this type of plant and creating reproducible systems that will help planters be effective in this pursuit, but it is a difficult path to follow if a planter wants to be financially supported in ministry. At this point we believe that bi-vocational planting or support from wealthy benefactors are some of the best paths for missionally-focused church planters.

Again, the common model is an attractional church, with a strong missional focus. This type of church puts energy into a quality public service which draws in people, but they equally focus on healthy small groups and service to the poor, marginalized and needy. So most planters will move into a community, gather a launch team that supports one another in Christian community and then launch a church with a public service. Six to nine months allows time for the planter to settle his family, get to know the community, etc.

Member churches of the church-planting network can hugely help the planter by assisting with the move itself, providing introductions, offering insights into the community and many other "little things" that make for a successful transition. A good move to the community is very important. Transitional tasks such as getting a family settled, helping get school registrations, phones, and mail forwarded to the new house are legitimate tasks for the planter in the first couple of weeks.

Step 10— The planter shares the vision in network churches

Network members should invite the planter to share the vision with their churches. This may be during weekend services, during special meetings or in staff meetings. Launch team members may surface during this vision-casting, so it is important for the network churches to clearly define any areas that are off limits for recruiting. This may include staff people, certain elders and certain members. The network churches should also be careful not to send "sick" members who will cause division or drag on a launch team.

In many plants in which the authors have been a participant a potential member has surfaced who didn't get his way in a previous congregation. One of the functions of the management team is to stand behind the planter as he confronts people who try to subvert the direction and vision of the plant and if necessary to step in and ask a person to leave. (This is a last resort. If the planter deals with the issue, it increases his leadership stature in the church plant.)

Step 11— The planter builds a team

The planter starts by building relationships and developing a community. Network churches also send resources and both long-term and short-term team members. The short-term "scaffolding people" are there to assist the building of the structure. One couple we know helped every church plant they could find establish its nursery. Once the nursery was set up and fully staffed, they left for the next plant.

Planters are often tempted to push a "grand opening" out as far in the future as possible, but it is financially a very expensive proposition. The management team needs to determine if a plant is ready to open in consultation with the planter and his coach. Sometimes delaying a start is valuable, but most often it just increases the up-front costs of the church plant. Most planters need to be pushed to develop their launch teams so they have at least fifty people (including kids) before launch, and they can launch within nine months.

Step 12—The church starts

Finally the church starts or the public launch takes place. Representatives of the network churches should attend the first services. This is important for two reasons: first, it is a reward for the hard-working network members who have devoted so much time and energy into launching the church. Nothing encourages them to consider a second plant like the energizing spirit of the first one coming to life! Second, the presence of network church leaders tells the new church it is not alone and lends credibility to the church in the eyes of first-time guests.

Today we encourage network churches, especially those at a distance, to also link with the new church via video or internet. This helps the many members of the network churches, who may be unable to attend the grand opening, to experience the excitement of launch. In 2011 a grand opening in Salt Lake City was attended by a network church via Skype as well as a network church attending in person.

Step 13—The planter receives ongoing coaching and support

Networks tend to sigh with relief and back off after launch. This is a mistake because, like any newborn, a new church needs support and training. It is extremely important for the management team to provide ongoing support for the planter. There will be conflicts, crises and tragedies. In an established church this is handled by elders or a leadership team. In a new church, if the management team doesn't provide this support, it is left on the shoulders of the planter.

The planter and his team should receive additional training outside the management team as well. The Exponential Conference, ChurchPlanters.com, NewThing and many other organizations provide training opportunities. At this point the planter should be invited to serve as a full participating partner in the church planting network or to help start a new network.

Most networks feel it is very important for new churches to reproduce within the first two to five years. By participating in the established network, the new church learns to collaborate and focus externally from the very beginning.

Step 14—We do it again!

After a short period of recovery, the network should begin planning its next plant. Many networks find it appropriate at this point to invite additional churches into the network. This gives the network new strength, provides fresh insights and moves the expansion of the kingdom to a new level. It is important that the network not lose the momentum that comes from a new church plant. It is always easier to maintain momentum than to return to a state of entropy and begin again.

In 2010, Stadia began to add a "glocal" dimension to the planting process. Now every network and new church is encouraged to plant an international church as their first act after the domestic church is planted. This gives the new church a global missions presence from the first day. It also provides an outlet for missional expression as well as transforming a community internationally.

****

We hope that this overview of our process is helpful. Seeing how the system works as a whole gives context to some of our specific policies and practices. The reader may want to review some of the documents that we use, which are provided for you in the appendices, to give the specifics behind some of our systems.

The process we described assumes that church leaders are in relationship and that they desire to plant churches together. We now want to describe how a coach guides and leads the network partners. We will than look at our general practice through three ways that I (Bobby) developed networks. We will then take a chapter to describe how we recruit and support leaders to through the 24-hour LEAD Team format.

11

COACHING STADIA'S NETWORKS

In this chapter:
- The roles and responsibilities of the network coach
- An in-depth glimpse at the systems and processes Stadia has developed
- An in-depth look at some of Stadia's infrastructure and processes

In this chapter we hope to clarify some of the roles and relationships in the leadership of our network system that were described in the last chapter. At Stadia we believe that the role of a network coach is critical to the success of a church-planting network and its progeny, a new daughter church. Networks are decentralized, but they still need a catalyst. In our network model the coach is the catalyst, the central figure in the church planting network.

There are several ways of leading. Some choose to dictate and some choose to lead without giving much direction, as two extremes. Those who dictate often tell people what to do. While this may seem quicker in the short term, no one learns much. Ownership of the project is minimal among the members of the network and the next time around the lessons will have to be learned again. There is also the risk that a network will not actually make it through the first plant. After all, a network is a voluntary association and people can vote with their feet. Usually when a highly dominant leader is "in charge" it is a one-time experience.

At the other end of the spectrum is a leader who just releases a group and assumes the people will figure it out. This method is akin to throwing a child into the water to teach them how to swim. They may survive, but the trauma may keep them out of the pool the rest of their life. This laissez-faire approach usually stems from either a lack of commitment to church planting or a leader who can only see the big picture and is not a strategic implementer.

Another option that is a little better than the first two is to lead by teaching. Early in the days when Stadia was still the Northern California Evangelistic Association (NCEA) we were asked to address various church-planting groups and church boards. We would go in, share what was working for us and then leave. Almost always things remained the same. The teaching of information is rarely adequate for a church-planting project to get off the ground. The weakness of this method of leading a church-planting network is that it is impossible to address all of the nuances and possible scenarios that may emerge in a church plant during a seminar.

Stadia believes that a coach/mentor for a network is crucial to the long term success of the network. Let us illustrate. When David Limiero came to Bakersfield he found declining churches and church splits were the norm and he pioneered a different approach. In partnership with the one church of any substance, Life Journey Christian Church was planted. After launch David was asked to be a network coach. David immediately drew the four pastors/ministers together into a network and began building relationships and establishing trust. Many of these churches had started out of splits from churches that had closed. The churches in the area had not done anything together in the past 30 years and all were in decline but one.

David began to cast vision for a second church. These small churches came together to plant Kaleo. Two years later they planted Plaza Iglesias Christiana. During this time one church merged with another congregation and rather than spend money on a new facility, they chose to use some of their funds to help plant the second and third church. They established an endowment that will continue to provide funds for church planting in their county.

David's role in this church-planting network cannot be overstated. Leading from an experience base David was able to quietly and confidently impart vision, draw partners in and help them navigate the hiring and coaching of two new plants. David fulfilled the role of both coach and mentor for the Kern County network.

A mentor is one who shares previous experiences so others can know what to do in the future. While no one's experience is 100 percent the same as another person's experience, the similarities of a mentor's experiences with those faced by the person following in his steps (in this case the network leaders) can help navigate the current situation.

A mentor is *someone who has gone ahead and pours back into someone else.* A coach is one who comes alongside a leader or a group of leaders and draws out. When we say, "draws out," what we mean is that the coach leads the group to express their thoughts together and clarify what they, not the coach, want to accomplish. The coach assumes that a person or group has had some experiences in the matter at hand that can be used as building blocks. Through them the coach enables the leader(s) to make decisions for themselves.[170] Mentors help through their experience; coaches help by asking questions so others can make their own decisions.

Every church-planting network can benefit from having a coach who is also a mentor to help the team along the way. The network coach is a catalyst. He pulls the network together, he educates the leaders on the process and then he empowers the leaders and coaches them so they make all the major decisions about the church plant project. In the end the network partners, often represented through the management team, own all the major decisions of the church plant project.

Besides wise counsel and asking the right questions, the network coach often provides energy to keep the process going forward. Planting a church requires a lot of energy and focus, especially when churches need to make financial contributions. Since network partners are often busy in their own rights, it sometimes falls on the coach to hold the team accountable for activities agreed upon together. The rubric, "Everyone's responsibility is no one's responsibility," holds true in networks. The coach must make sure that someone is taking responsibility for the issues facing the team.

The roles of recruiter, mentor and coach are the most important functions the coach will fulfill over the long term. As a network begins to work on their second and third plants, the advisor role will somewhat lessen since the members of the network have the knowledge and experience. They have walked the path before, but the keeper of accountability will remain the same. Additionally, as the network adds new members, the coach will need to help them get up to the same level of experience and knowledge as the original members.

Network Coach Responsibilities

The coach must be good at relationships because relationships are the basis by which he connects with and invites church leaders to hear about the vision and possibilities. When I (Bobby) first started recruiting and looking for network coaches in the East, finding a relational person was our first priority. I looked for men who were respected leaders, knowledgeable about church planting and very good at relational connections. God blessed me with a great team, starting with several church planters that I had coached and Doug Fultz, a ministry colleague, who was leading a church three miles from mine. Here is a summary of the network coach's job description that we developed:

1. Develop relationships with Independent Christian Churches/Churches of Christ in the area – or within the agreed upon parameters - in order to cast the vision and build a team which will develop a church planting network.
2. Hold meetings with the ministers/pastors of the region – or within the parameters - to create passion and vision for church planting in the area.
3. Become a student in the craft of church planting through the network.
4. Lead potential network participants through a process that results in a signed Memorandum of Understanding (M.O.U.) which describes the exact commitment each of the parties will make to form a network that plants a church, collaborates in ministry and is mutually supportive.
5. Lead the network to form a management team and hire a church planter.

6.   Lead in developing new sites and strategies for planting more and more churches.

7.   Work closely with Stadia's Mobilization Team in developing up to three networks and be creative to make the church planting network ever increasingly effective.

8.   Meet monthly by phone with an assigned director, interact regularly with other CPN coaches and file a written monthly report that documents activity and outcomes of work.

There are some elements within the responsibilities of a network coach which are particularly important. We want to highlight these elements and explain why they are important.

Recruit Network Partners

The first task of the network coach is to relationally connect with the leaders of local churches or other network partners. The goal is to establish rapport and invite them to learn about and consider joining the network. We will describe this process in more detail in the next chapter, but to understand the role of a network coach, it is important to understand his role as recruiter. Without the coach as a catalyst and recruiter, the network would not form by itself. We have said it throughout this book, and we say it again: relationships are fundamental to everything in a network. As Tom Jones repeatedly tells us, "It's all about relationships."

One of the best ways to start a network is with a twenty-four hour gathering. The coach is the catalyst for the twenty-four hour retreat. The levels of trust and vision that are built during one guided twenty-four hour period are phenomenal. More can be accomplished in one twenty-four hour period than in six months of one or two hour meetings. As new network members are added, it is important for the new members and the older members to have these opportunities to dream together and establish trust.

The Kingdom Synergy Partnership network in Ohio repeats these twenty-four hour retreats annually and finds great value for both new and old members. I (Marcus) recently attended one of their twenty-four hour retreats. Leaders from the partner churches, church planters and church-planters-in-training gathered to pray and plan. The tone was set by a very candid time of sharing and praying for one another. Issues that the leaders were struggling with were shared and prayed for. Two planters who had not yet planted were prayed for specifically and both of them have now gone on to start churches through the network.

They spent time looking at places that needed new churches in their region and suggested strategies for the next plants. I also spent some time troubleshooting issues with current plants. Since twenty-four hour retreats do not happen without intentionality, the coach plans, recruits people to join and leads these retreats. These retreats are enjoyable times away from the hustle and bustle of church life and help forge relationships and inspire network partners.

Cast the Vision and Lead the Process

Next to recruiting, the second most important task of the network coach is to cast vision (and educate the leaders). The vision for reaching and transforming lost people through church planting is that which captures the imagination. As we have built networks, there are several tools that are useful in casting the vision for a new Network.

First, testimonies from other networks and from church planters help the people get excited about working together to plant a church. The power of story is close to irresistible in drawing people together. As Stadia has adopted the view that our product is not new churches but transformed lives and communities, we have made a point of telling the stories of life change and community transformation. We regularly gather anecdotal evidence and testimonies about what God is doing.

Second, it is often necessary to establish the need for new churches. Sometimes pastors or leaders may claim that there are already too many churches. Dave Olson, Ed Stetzer, Tom Nebel and many others have built a compelling case for the decline of Christian influence in our society. Even many pastors are unaware that the number of churches per capita has been steadily declining for the past 50 years. Statistics are very helpful.

Third, Stadia uses MissionInsite, a church-focused demographic service, to help networks understand the needs of the community and the type of planter who will be effective in leading a new church to address them. An oft quoted though old statistic from the American Institute of Church Growth is that a community with a church/population ratio of greater than one church per 1000 people is

under-churched. Rarely in the U.S. do we find a community with this ration and on the coasts and northern edge of the North America the ratio is often one church per 2500 people or more.

Once the vision has been clearly cast and the process has been outlined and explained to the network partners, the network coach leads them – step-by-step – through the process. Since we have already outlined the process in an earlier chapter, we will not cover it again at this point. There are some key elements in the Stadia process, however, which deserve special highlights.

Minimum Standards and Types of Churches

Stadia is committed to upholding seven minimum standards to ensure that church plants have the best chance of succeeding. We covered these in the last chapter, so we will not repeat them here. We want to describe how a coach helps a network determine the type of church it wants to plant and then to navigate this decision through our seven minimum standards.

As the network partners begin meeting and catching the vision, with the help of the coach (and others), they will be led to make a commitment. The commitment is a covenant or Memorandum of Understanding (MOU) which outlines these minimum standards and other parts of the network church-planting project (see a sample MOU in the appendices). Please be aware that these documents are live documents and are constantly changing. They may also not fit every single network and will almost always need to be modified in some ways for a specific church plant.

One of the most important decisions that must be made is the type of church that will be planted. I (Bobby) was responsible for training most of Stadia's planters up until just recently. We have planted six basic types of churches as of spring 2011 (and variations of each one). It is important for each network to be clear about the type of church that they want to plant, because there are strengths and weaknesses inherent in each model.

- Purpose Driven Church – this is typically a traditional type of church with strong Sunday morning programming. The focus is excellence in preaching, praise and worship, and children's ministry. It is also typically an expensive model, requiring financial support for staff who can provide the programming excellence.

- Organic Church – often called a "house church," this model is much less expensive than the Purpose Driven model. The focus is leadership for house churches, where the planter develops and multiplies house churches. This is a fluid model, as each "house church" tends to have a short life and tremendous fluidity.

- Cell Church – this is a model of church that is popular in Asia and South America and has been developed with effectiveness in some North American contexts. The focus is upon small groups and the leadership of small groups. Typically a planter will start five to seven small groups and then start a regular Sunday gathering. Because there is so much emphasis on small groups, there is often a perceived rigidity in this model and it may not be as effective with more educated people who tend to be very busy and authority resistant.

- Missional Church – In theory, many young leaders prefer this model. It seems to capture their hearts and imaginations, as it focuses on reaching those on the margins and the poor. Yet, at present, it is not a well-developed model. There are promising signs and hopeful missional church plant projects, but much work is yet to be done to develop a reproducible model that is sustainable in the long run.

- Simple Church – often loosely based upon the book *Simple Church*, by Thom Rainer and Eric Gieger, this model seeks to develop a "discipleship process" based upon a balance of Sunday services, small groups, and service to the community.[171] In many ways, a hybrid of this model, with a strong Sunday gathering and missional communities that serve the community is currently the most popular. The tricky part is developing an effective church which is so labor intensive – it takes tremendous leadership and energy to provide programming excellence, development of community between Christians, and effective service of the community.

- Relational Discipleship Church – this model is utilized by Real Life Ministries in Post Falls, Idaho. It is a model which seems to pull together the strengths of all the others models – serving the community, quality Sunday programming, small groups, and a strong emphasis on discipleship. This model is currently producing churches with exceptionally high growth rates – and a highly positive impact upon the communities where these churches are

planted. Jim Putman has articulated these principles in his books; *Church is a Team Sport*, *Real Life Discipleship*, and *Real Life Discipleship Training Manual*. The model is a deceptively different way of doing church. On the surface, it seeks to create a discipleship model based upon Jesus and the gospels, but with such a heavy emphasis on *agape* love and relationships, it requires an entirely new way of approaching ministry.

Network coaches typically guide the network partners through the different models. It is their role to guide the network to make the best decision. In some cases, a decision on the type of church to be planted will be put off, because the network partners want the church planter to lead with the model he prefers.

Once the MOU has been signed, the network will be encouraged to form a smaller "working" group called the Management Team. Usually all churches who contribute significantly are invited to have a place on the management team. By helping the network partners choose people who can work together and have the time and inclination to be part of the management team, the coach can help set the team up for success.

Often the tendency will be to choose the most dominant person in the network as the management team chair; however, the person who can facilitate and bring out the best, especially in the church planter, is the right choice. Since the first order of business of the management team is to choose a chairperson and adopt guidelines for the team, the coach is in a primary position to help that happen.

Stadia provides training and coaching for the chairman of the management team. John Wasem, our director of management teams, is very knowledgeable and experienced in this area. In partnership with the network coach, John makes sure that the management team chairman will have the needed resources, management team guidelines and understanding of what it takes to be a successful management team chairperson.

The Management Team is in Charge of the Project

It is important for the management team to have ownership of the church plant project. After choosing a location, deciding on a planter profile and seeking a candidate, the next best practice that

needs to be followed is the pre-assessment and assessment process. Again, the network coach and management team coach, with a greater knowledge of where assessment services can be procured and how to interpret the results of the assessment, will play a key role in advising the management team. One of the most important parts of the hiring process is for all members of the management team to express their approval or disapproval of a particular candidate. A good management team chairman will see that everyone is heard and that all concerns are expressed.

The management team's most important job is to find a quality church-planting couple. The lead planter (and spouse) is the singular most important factor in the success of the church plant. This is another area, in our experience, where the adage, "Everything rises and falls on leadership," is demonstrably true. Their second most important job is supporting the lead planter couple once they have been hired.

If a planter candidate is not home grown, the network coach's connections with Stadia or other church planting associations or both are often important in locating potential planters. Because of Stadia's reputation and national presence, Stadia is often aware of candidates that a network may not know. It is advisable in most cases for a member of the management team or for the planter coach to attend the assessment center to see and feel firsthand what the assessment team is finding. This will pay dividends farther down the road in improved coaching and in building some safeguards for the planter in areas of particular weakness.

Strategy and Finances

As described in the previous chapter, as soon as the planter passes assessment, Stadia invites the planter, spouse and team to come to bootcamp for training. Starting in the fall of 2010, Stadia is now doing our training "in house." This training guides a planter and his team through all the major biblical and strategic issues involved in a church plant project. When they come out of bootcamp, every church plant team will have a strategic and financial plan. These plans must be approved by the management team.

Planters are dreamers and usually have huge visions for what can be accomplished. This is a wonderful thing. The management team will review the strategic plan and help serve as a reality check.

Management teams should only focus on major areas of disagreement. It displays bad leadership if a management team gets focused on the minute details.

Since the management team is also responsible for the oversight of finances, having an approved plan is key. Many planters have destroyed a plant with unwise spending based on decisions made in the heat of battle rather than by following a plan of many counselors.

In conjunction with the financial plan, a professional church plant bookkeeper should be employed unless one of the network partners has an accounting department with professional bookkeepers as part of their church. In most cases Stadia has found that it is best to have an outside professional do the books. This provides accountability, it takes the planter off of the checkbook and provides lines of communication on a regular basis to the management team chair, the coach and the planter.

Regularly we see volunteer bookkeepers who, though well-intentioned, miss payments, improperly receipt donations or allow the planter to push them into unwise spending practices. My (Marcus) mantra for the church planter is, "There are two ways you can ruin your church plant – become involved with another woman or improperly use money entrusted to you. Either one will shoot your church plants in the foot."

The Planter's Coach

In the best case scenario, a church plant couple and their team will go to bootcamp with a personal coach for the church planter. Stadia helps the planter and management team procure the services of a planter coach simultaneously with bootcamp. In Stadia's case there is a cadre of professionally trained coaches who are available to networks. There are times when a network will choose to train one of its own members as the planter coach. If this choice is made the network coach can help in the selection of a suitable coach. Again the network coach's connection to Stadia helps facilitate these choices.

The choice of a coach for the planter is somewhat personal. There must be a "clicking" between planter and coach if there is going to be open and healthy interchange on an ongoing basis. Stadia prefers coaches who seek to draw out of the planter that which he already knows but may be afraid to express or may be procrastinating on accomplishing or both.

A coach that is too directive will try to plant "his" church plant and accomplish "his" vision rather than helping the planter realize God's will for his life and plant. There is a balance here because the planter must plant God's church, one that is grounded first and foremost in what the Bible teaches and the principles which Jesus modeled.

Good coaching is essential. A coach who is afraid to confront will allow a planter to make unchallenged decisions that may either be thoughtless or ill advised. Many of these decisions will be the result of inexperience as many planters have never walked this path before. A coach who asks probing questions and calls the planter to be accountable to the goals which the planter has set will help the planter avoid many crashes.

Stadia has found that a wildly successful "one plant phenomenon" is less effective as a coach than someone who has struggled along the way. Most planters will struggle so having a coach who can be touched by their struggles is infinitely helpful. At times the coach might be forced to be directive in an emergency or when facing repeated refusals to choose the right path.

An agreement between the coach, the management team and the planter will establish guidelines and frequency for coaching. Stadia requires coaching reports on a monthly basis to be provided to the management team chair, the network coach and the director of planter care. Coaching stipend is not paid until the report is submitted.

One of the cooperative jobs of the management team chair and Stadia is to see that adequate coaching is taking place and neither the planter nor the coach is letting it slip. It is often easy for the coaching appointments to be missed due to the busyness of life in a church plant. Once that becomes a pattern, it is very difficult to regain the coaching relationship.

Project Management

Stadia provides a project manager for every church plant. The project manager ensures that the church planter covers all the details in the project. He is an expert in the details who serves almost as part time staff for the planter leading up to the launch of the church.

Many church leaders who have never planted a church do not realize how many details must be covered and the amount of time and energy that can be wasted without the guidance of project management. The project manager serves as the communication bridge between the planter, coach and Management team chair. He also helps develop expectations and key vitals of health for the project. Those are then used to monthly evaluate the health of the project.

There are usually 150 to 180 major tasks that must be accomplished between the time a planter is hired and time for the grand opening. It may include developing logos, creating websites, securing legal issues such as incorporation and obtaining a 501(c)(3) designation from the IRS, obtaining benefits for the planter's family, finding staff and volunteers, developing ministry guidelines, finding a facility, purchasing a sound system, and establishing small group curriculum. Many planters are not detail oriented, but are rather more spontaneous and people persons, so having a project manager is vital.

Prior to the establishment of Project Management Systems it was often the norm for numerous items to be passed over and frantically accomplished at the last minute. Most of the time this scramble was at great cost to family harmony for the planter and caused unnecessary conflicts or excessively costly expenditures and often resulted in penalties due to lack of compliance.

While the management team may not understand the importance of the project management system at first, we have found that as they walk with the planter through the process, they become raving fans. The network may want to provide some of the services for the plant in order to save money, but this is usually a needless distraction. The network coach can help them determine which services will actually help and which will not be suitable for a new plant. Again the prior experience of the network coach is invaluable at this point.

Spousal Care

It is vitally important that we provide support for the spouses of church planters. The management team will want to regularly check on the family of the planter. A planter's spouse is often lonely and has no one to turn to. Since many times a planter will use his home as the church office for planning meetings and a general drop-in center, it is important that someone listens to the spouse for signs of bad boundaries and marital conflict.

Stadia has developed a program called *Bloom!* for the spouses of lead church planters. Led by Debbie Jones this is a vital ministry that focuses upon support and encouragement. Wives who were previously on the fence have become big fans of Stadia. *Bloom!* meets together in retreats, in chat rooms and in coffee shops. Regular communications and notes of support as well as reminders to planters (such as "Remember Valentine's Day is coming.") help the planter wives remain encouraged and enthusiastic participants in the church plant.

In the years since its inception, Stadia has found that *Bloom!* is one of our best recruiting and planter care tools but wise network leaders and management teams do not rely only on Bloom!. They regularly check in on their church planters and spouses and make sure that they are receiving the highest level of support and encouragement.

Director of Mobilization and Church Planting Networks

The formation of Stadia networks is led by our Associate Executive Director of Mobilization, Brent Foulke. Brent's role is to see that networks are being developed around the country and that existing networks are starting new projects after their current plants are "on their own." Obviously it is too big a job for one person, so Stadia has recruited 4 associate network directors to lead more or less the 4 quadrants of the US. Each of the associate network directors encourages churches and pastors in their regions to join together into networks and then sees that network coaches are provided for each of the networks. The network coaches then take the role of helping lead the network into fruitfulness. By delegating and decentralizing, Stadia is able to cover a much wider area with less cost than having a few full time leaders running as fast as they can in all directions.

The work of catalyzing is much the same at every level. Often I (Marcus) or Brent Foulke will go to a new area with only one or two interested churches and have a few conversations to scout the relational landscape. The first priority is figuring out which leaders already have existing relationships in the region and the best person to bring others into the network. A close second priority is understanding the demographics and need of an area .

After Brent or myself (Marcus) have an introductory meeting the goal is to pave the way for the associate network director in the region or a new network coach to continue the building of trust and relationships and ultimately to call the network into existence. Since all of our Associate Network Directors are less than 10 hours per week, Brent does much of the scouting and initial contacting in order to maximize his time and influence. Soon a fledgling network is being formed and the mission of the kingdom is being advanced.

Networks all begin, we must remember, with a relationship between church leaders. That relationship is solidified through support, learning, and the mission to plant churches. It can seem like a difficult thing to start micro-networks from scratch, but if a coach is patient, a network can be built without much difficulty. In the next chapter we will describe three typical ways that we do it.

12

STARTING MICRO-NETWORKS

In this chapter:
- How we start micro-networks
- How apostolic leaders help micro-network coaches
- How you can help start or join a network

It is important to remember that national or macro networks cover a broad geographic region like Acts 29, ARC or Converge do. They function as a national platform for church planting resources and church planters. The macro network has national or apostolic leaders who cast the vision and promote the DNA of the network over multiple channels. These leaders are visible and often well-known. In reality, however, they do not make the biggest practical impact within networks. The network coach is the point man and catalyst for the local or micro network. Local or micro networks function in a specific locality or with a specific relational hub.

One of the biggest barriers leaders often face when starting local micro networks are the *How* questions. We have tried to answer most of these questions up to this point in the book. How do local networks work? How do the leaders learn about church planting? How does the network find a church planter? How does the planter get training?

At this point many may ask the biggest question of all--how do you start a local micro network? In this chapter we would like to describe three different ways that we have created micro-networks within the Stadia system. These three are cited as models for illustrative purposes to show the reader how micro networks can be created. As you read through our descriptions of these models please bear in mind that behind the various activities are four fundamental principles – pray, focus on relationships, cast the vision of reaching lost people and celebrate what God does.

1. Build Your Own Church Planting Micro-network.

When I (Bobby) was first introduced to the network model, even before Stadia adopted it on a national scale, I was immediately persuaded about its merits. I felt that I should build a local network among our Christian churches in my area. I live in the Nashville, Tennessee, area and we had seven or eight churches in our tribe. Some of the churches that I contacted were mid-to-large-sized churches and others were relatively small. Some of the partners were church plants and some were churches that had been around for many years.

I started the process by developing deeper relationships with the senior ministers/pastors of these churches. Some of us had met on occasions before to encourage each other and share resources. I began the process of making sure our meetings were regular and then I invited each of the leaders to make sure they attended these meetings. In the process we developed relationships, shared resources and I started to cast the vision for planting churches.

I showed them, through graphs and charts, that we could plant a lot of churches in the upcoming years if we worked together. By explaining the power of shared resources with specific numerical targets, everyone started to see what we could accomplish. The biggest selling point for everyone was the individual church-planting stories we shared, often through videos or special guests. As we saw these stories of transformed lives and transformed communities everyone caught the vision.

In this way I was the first network coach. I saw my role as being the intentional leader who recruited everyone, cast the vision and asked these men to take the message back to their leaders so their churches could join with us. Because these concepts were new for many of the leaders, it took numerous lunch-time gatherings and breakfasts over numerous months before sufficient levels of trust and energy were built. Because of the sizes of the churches and the newness of the concept, it required the involvement of the senior leader of each of the churches.

In most churches, if the senior minister/pastor is not on board, the church will not have traction with church planting and they will not truly support the micro network. But when he is truly on board, he will lead the leaders of the church to get behind the project. Then when the other leaders of the church become involved, the whole church begins to develop a shared commitment to the network and the process of planting churches.

The relationship-building phase typically comes first. Micro networks are all about relationships first and the Kingdom mission is built out of the relationship. In order to initiate the relationships, I found that it was sometimes necessary to seek referrals and or introductions from one senior leader to another. In the earliest days of our Nashville area micro network, I formed a good friendship with fellow lead minister/pastor Doug Fultz and he helped recruit other senior ministers/pastors with me.

While focusing on building supportive relationships and sharing resources for ministry, I also made sure that we built a foundation for the micro network as a partnership in mission. This phase of a new network may take quite a bit of time, but my role was to make sure that we did not get discouraged at the lack of progress as we built consensus and a commitment to partner together.

As you develop a network it may also be necessary to "go with the goers" at this point. Some leaders are happy to talk about planting churches but they are not really committed to making it happen. Others are threatened or "too busy" or have a host of other reasons for not being a part. If you wait until every person has signed on in a given area, you may never get started. It is better to begin once a sufficient core is gathered, and then add others over time, than it is to wait until every single church is represented.

As the network begins to have success, more leaders will join in. It will be important to develop an attitude of welcoming because you will have formerly recalcitrant partners who will be "converted" to church planting after the micro networks start to demonstrate fruit. A wise network leader will take advantage of those who want to jump on the bandwagon after momentum develops. Though it can be tough to see some people claiming victory, those who joined at the last minute, remember that the goal is to plant more churches and those coming late to the table bring increased resources and sometimes renewed energy.

Once enough church leaders and their churches were on board, I knew it was time to hold a commitment discussion. To get ready for the commitment discussion I had previously explained the exact process churches follow to find the exact location for the church, the planter to plant the church and the best model to be used. The network partners would make these decisions together and this shared ownership would be critical moving forward. They also came to understand the importance of assessing potential church planters, church planter bootcamps and coaching (key principles for Stadia). I also explained the cost breakdown for the new church so that everyone knew exactly how the money was going to be spent and the total contribution needed from each church.

The commitment meeting is the most significant event in the network. I took time to equip each leader so that he would be able to come to the meeting with the full support of his home church. I encouraged these leaders to bring a number of other leaders (especially key staff members or elders). This would enable them to go back to their congregations with more momentum than if they did it just by themselves.

The network coach must be prepared for additional unexpected meetings with key leaders until they can make a decision. It is helpful to make sure that everyone is ready to sign before they arrive at the meeting. Expect some dropouts at this point but don't let it slow you down. It is important to "go with the goers".

At this meeting we utilized a Memorandum Of Understanding (MOU) or a covenant. This is a written document that outlines the specific commitments each congregation would be making and the specific practices we would uphold (Stadia's key practices). This was an exciting meeting when we cast the vision of the future church, described our appreciation for each other and then took a picture that will be shared with each of our churches and hopefully shared with the participants of the new church once it is started.

After signing, be sure to conclude the time with some prayer of thanksgiving to God and allow people to express their excitement and commitment to the process. Since the MOU will include the financial commitments of the churches, it is important to have instructions for the church bookkeepers with firm, clear dates set for all payments to the partnership. Even though clear instructions are given, be prepared to follow up and make sure that all money comes into the proper account.

The network coach at this point needs to set a date for the next meeting and lead the group through the rest of the process. This process is described in detail in previous chapters, but is also summarized as follows:

1. Determining the exact location of the plant.
2. Developing a clear job description/profile for the planter.
3. Setting up the management team.
4. Coaching the management team on the process of hiring the planter.
5. Ensuring that a chairman of the management team is appointed and trained, so that he can guide the group through the rest of the process.
6. Being available to the management team for help if unforeseen difficulties arise.

The most difficult part of building a micro network from scratch like this comes in the early days. The network coach must be very persistent and patient. It takes time to develop relationships and to cast the vision of planting churches through a network when the potential partners have few references or background understanding of how the process works.

2. Follow an Apostolic Leader and Pull Together a Micro Network

It is easier to establish a micro network when you can follow a respected national leader who opens the door for the process. Once Stadia embraced the network model, Marcus Bigelow would travel around the country, gather church leaders together and cast the vision. Marcus Bigelow opened the door for me (Bobby) to start a church-planting network in Indianapolis because he brought together a group of senior ministers/pastors from the area that already knew and respected Marcus and Stadia. Marcus was the visionary recruiter who initiated the network by telling the story of other networks and casting the vision for the potential micro network in Indiana.

The InNetwork is now statewide with dozens of churches working together, but in the early days it was only a few key pastors who met with us. Again, the importance of relationships both in the formation and in the working of a network cannot be overstated. After a couple of individual meetings, two of the pastors helped Marcus issue invitations to those we had good relationships with. We met in a Holiday Inn meeting room and six key leaders from Indianapolis showed up. These men went home excited and ready to meet again.

Prior to these meetings, Marcus recruited me (Bobby) to serve as the network coach to follow up and create the micro network, so we met together with the leaders of five large independent Christian churches. We got to know each other and Marcus cast the vision of what they could do together. At the conclusion of this introductory meeting I gained a commitment from all present to meet again with a time and place agreed upon. It was much easier to start this kind of network because the leaders already had relationships with each other and Marcus was able to show them the broad vision of how the network model was the future for how Stadia was going to plant churches.

It was a little difficult for Marcus to "let go" of the group. When you build relationships you naturally want to see it come to a successful conclusion, however, I (Bobby) took it much farther than Marcus would have been able to take it. The success of this endeavor points to a key learning. There is a difference between a national vision caster and a catalyst. Marcus brought people together and built some energy, and I took that energy and channeled it into a smoothly-functioning church-planting network. Both brought necessary skills to the table—Marcus was the national vision-caster and I was the hands on coach.

One of the frustrating experiences for some of Marcus' co-workers is the ease with which Marcus can step into a situation and bring people to the table in a very short time while the coach may have been struggling to pull the group together for months. Utilizing a team approach to building networks is vital. National leaders have the ability, because of their profile, to pull people together. Wise network coaches will utilize this ability whenever the opportunity presents itself

Following this meeting as a network coach, it was my responsibility for follow-up and the scheduling of future meetings. In this model the visionary is responsible for vision casting and the network coach is responsible for the strategic implementation of a plan. Like other micro networks, the foundation is twofold: 1) a desire for relationship/partnership among leaders/churches and 2) the planting of a church. Because the visionary is a peer who is taking a lead role, it sometimes takes additional time to build relationships and gain trust among the members. When the going is slow, both the visionary leader and the network coach must remember the long-term possibilities that can be accomplished through this network.

As additional people and churches are recruited, it may be necessary to "repeat" the first meeting with the newcomers so that everyone is able to get on board. Soon the momentum moves closer to the point of decision and action. When a sufficient number of leaders are clearly interested, the network coach schedules a meeting to talk about a commitment to planting. As with the other models of building a network, the original leader from the church is encouraged to bring additional leaders and staff from his church to gain buy-in on a wider level.

At this meeting a general MOU should be introduced and the participants asked to take the material back to their staff and/or elders. The network coach should clearly indicate that he will be following up in two or three weeks to see how the staff and elders have responded. It may be necessary for the network coach to meet with the elders and staff of several churches in order to cast vision for church planting.

After there is some clear commitment to the network, the date should be set for a meeting at which the MOU or covenant will be signed. It must be made clear that this is a signing meeting and not a further discussion meeting. At the same time, the network coach and the visionary leader must be prepared for additional delays and unexpected meetings. This may be frustrating especially for the visionary leader who is already well down the road to planting.

The "behind the scenes dynamics" in other churches are not always apparent and many times remain hidden behind the insecurities or the inability of a leader to move his staff and/or elders forward. The coach must be ready to smooth ruffled feathers and encourage those who are becoming discouraged with the lack of progress.

The visionary leader and the network coach must be aware that most of the time the behind the scenes politics and maneuvering will not be revealed. The real reasons given for not participating or for "foot dragging" are usually not expressed up front. Gentle and loving probing may reveal the true cause of what is really happening "back home." Only by taking the time to build relationships and trust can the network proceed forward and solve the problems that keep a specific church from participating.

As in our other model, the most significant concrete step in the forward direction of the network is when the leaders commit to planting a church through the signing of an MOU or covenant. As in other networks, once the MOU has been signed it becomes the duty of the network coach to lead the group through the rest of the process.

3. Partner with a Macro Network and Pull Together a Micro Network

Stadia is a macro network of micro networks. Stadia also partners with other like-minded macro networks within our fellowship of churches. One of the most effective partnerships that Stadia has developed is with a macro network of independent Christian Churches in Ohio. The Kingdom Synergy Partnership came together for (the following is their official statement) *the express purpose of exponentially expanding God's kingdom through synergy partnerships that were relentlessly committed to multiplying healthy growing churches.*

Under the leadership and vision of Greg Nettle, healthy mega-churches, healthy smaller churches, Cincinnati Christian University, the Center for church advancement, NOAH (a local church planting network), Stadia and others came together to support their vision--stated succinctly and with force: "Make It Hard to Go to Hell in Ohio."

Greg was awakened in the middle of the night for a couple of hours. He began writing what he sensed was the vision of God for his life and for Northern Ohio churches. After some refinement, he brought this to a group of fellow leaders and shared the vision.

The specific vision involved two distinct processes. First, churches were to help other churches to grow and develop spiritual health. To do this several healthy mega-churches would each enter into a mentoring role with two smaller churches that were in the process of breaking growth barriers. This mentoring role would include building relationships among senior pastors, church staffs and church elder boards. These folks would meet together several times each year for three years to help the emerging mega-churches grow. At the end of three years it was envisioned that each of the members of the triad would assume the mentoring role with two additional churches each.

The second part of the vision was for groups of churches to work together and take responsibility to plant churches. Stadia was invited to join with the Kingdom Synergy Partnership (KSP) to provide expertise in church-planting networks and church planting. Looking back over the last five years, our partnership with the KSP Macro network is one of the most exciting developments among all our networks.

At the beginning of KSP, Greg invited me (Marcus) to come to a meeting and share how Stadia might come alongside the churches in Ohio. Attended by over 100 pastors, associate staff and elders and deacons, this meeting created a large amount of excitement and energy. Most people signed on shortly afterward but a few just went home. This re-emphasizes the need to let some people go in order to focus on those who are ready to move forward. Greg made it clear that he and his home church were going to keep on moving and though they were hopeful that others would join with them, it was still going to happen.

The next step really follows the Indiana model in that a group was gathered for education and commitment. In the early part of this relationship a lot of time was spent persuading the leaders on the value of church planting and the network advantage for church planting. Even though the leaders had made a commitment, most did not understand the principles involved and how things would work. Greg Nettle gathered the leaders of the churches together and I (Bobby) provided training for everyone on the process and cast vision for what could be accomplished.

We brought in church planters who would tell their stories and provide inspiration for all in attendance. I was just developing the process described in chapter ten and, although it was faster than building a network from scratch, it still took a significant amount of time. As an apostolic leader with wide respect, Greg Nettle also helped bring all the partners along by the example that he and his church provided. They were always the first to state publicly their commitment to projects and the exact amount of money they were going to put up for each new church.

With the example of Greg and his church, River Tree Christian Church, many others were quick to join in with them. The first church plant project was time consuming and required a lot of patience and prayer. But soon the mission of planting churches became a part of all the discussion at all gatherings of the KSP network.

The first church was planted and celebrated, then the second, then the third and soon momentum was growing. It has now been five years. At the most recent KSP network gathering, $600,000 was committed from network partners for church planting. The momentum, under Greg's inspired commitment and encouragement, is now creating a state-wide kingdom impact. The network partners are creating new network hubs in Cleveland and Cincinnati. Greg and I (Bobby) recently met and summarized the progress to date, under God's guidance.

1. Twelve high-impact churches will have been planted by the end of the fifth year of the KSP's existence, and financial commitments are in place for six more;
2. The mentoring role within the churches has produced significant gains for church growth among the emerging churches;
3. The relationships and partnerships are spreading over into other projects such as strong participation in Compassion International and other mission endeavors.

This model is being shared with key leaders in other states with a desire to promote the same type of partnership in regions that have numbers of mega-churches that are willing to become mentor churches.

Summary

Developing micro networks is initially a slow process, but over time, with vision casting, education and a focus on relationship development, they become more and more effective. It is especially helpful for national or apostolic leaders to cast the vision about the benefits of planting churches through networks. It is more effective when there are regional macro networks with leaders who cast vision, model commitment and call others to join with them. We hope and pray that God will raise up countless Greg Nettles around the country. These men are of incalculable value in establishing and developing micro networks.

Here are some of the things that we have learned along the way:

1. Someone must always cast the vision for a new network-- sometimes it is a regional or national leader and sometimes it is a local network coach or catalytic leader.
2. Networks come together much faster when both national leaders and network coaches are utilized.
3. Network coaches are essential because they follow up on the details and operational work of a network. Regional or national leaders are typically too busy for this follow up.
4. Relationships take time to build but are the foundation for any functional network.

It is important to involve churches of various sizes in a network in order to cast a wide vision for church planting.

One of the best ways to start and maintain a healthy micro-network is through the 24-Hour Gathering we have referred to several times. Because this model is so helpful for building relationships, training, and making decisions, the final chapter will explore it in detail.

13

THE 24-HOUR LEADER GATHERING

In this chapter:
- The dynamics of 24-hour gatherings
- An hour-by-hour description of the 24-hour gatherings
- How you can start or join a 24-hour gathering

One of the most enjoyable learning experiences of my (Bobby) life was a 24-hour gathering held in the Nashville area in 2007. At the time I was seeking to learn all I could about coaching leaders and I was in dialogue with other leaders around the U.S. and Canada about how to train and certify coaches of church-planters. Three of the leaders of Converge Worldwide were a part of the discussion and they graciously agreed to join with me and a few other leaders to show us how they created, equipped and nurtured local networks (micro networks) of leaders who coached each other through what they called "24 hour Lead Team Meetings."

Tom Nebel, Gary Rohrmayer, and Paul Johnson flew to Nashville where several others joined with us in the experience commonly used by Converge to 1) form networks, 2) create church plants and 3) coach church planters and leaders. This 24-hour "LEAD Team Meeting," as they call it, is a key by which Converge Worldwide functions as both a denomination and a network. *The 24-hour LEAD team meetings are the backbone by which they were able to double in size in a twenty-year period.*

According to national authority, Ed Stetzer, *there is no other major denomination or organization that has done anything like this in North America in recent times.*[172] I knew I was going to learn a lot. I found the gathering to be so helpful and inspirational that I immediately started using it to help other leaders around the country to form local networks in the Stadia system.

The name, "LEAD" team, is based on an acronym.

L – "Learn,"
E – "Encourage,"
A – "Achieve,"
D – "Dream."

The acronym sums up what happens at the twenty-four hour gathering – leaders learn about church planting and coaching, they encourage each other in their personal and ministry lives, they achieve through their planning together and they dream of ongoing church planting works. Since the "LEAD Team" format is now commonly used to gather and build local networks in the Stadia system, we thought that our readers would find it helpful for us to describe, in detail, how the gathering works and the benefits that are found through it.

We will describe the gathering in its most basic form, trusting the reader to understand that there will be variations depending on the needs and plans of specific Stadia networks. We believe that this gathering is an ideal combination of relationship building and support, learning, shared experience, coaching, dreaming and action. Because it is an intense twenty-four hour period, it enables church leaders to come together at an in-depth level. It gives church leaders an opportunity to get away from their daily duties long enough to experience support from other leaders, significant learning and decision making about church planting in a highly relational environment. Yet because it is just twenty-four hours every two months, it is *just one day away* from their busy ministries. We have found that, once they see the value, most ministers and pastor can find a way to commit to it.

The Three "Dynamics" Behind the 24-Hour LEAD Team Gathering

The tag line in the introductory training slide for LEAD Team meetings says it all: "Relationships worth building and dreams worth chasing". Originally these gatherings were designed just for church-planting coaches, but they soon evolved to include key leaders from local churches who believed in church planting and wanted to attend to learn and join in the process. Soon these gatherings became a means by which local church leaders and their churches actively participated in church planting. Previously they had a passive support to church planting.

There are three key dynamics in a LEAD Team gathering: *relational, spiritual and missional.* The relational dynamic, as we have stated throughout this book, is key to micro networks. One of biggest insights for those who are not involved in full time ministry is to learn how lonely and isolated ministry leaders can feel. Often those who are involved in volunteer leadership in the local church – those serving as deacons or elders for example – think they understand and empathize with those in full time ministry but they simply cannot. Until you experience, on a daily basis, the spiritual and emotional warfare involved in full time ministry over a period of months and years, you cannot fully empathize with those who do experience it.

When Paul told Timothy to join him in serving like a good soldier in 2 Timothy 2:3, he was speaking volumes to everyone in full time ministry. This is one of the reasons why church leaders love the LEAD Team meetings – they share, at a deep level, both their ministries and life with peers who are experiencing the same life they are experiencing.

I (Bobby) have been in these overnight gatherings with leaders from all parts of North America, leaders from churches with 100 in attendance to leaders from churches with over 13,000 in attendance and the stories are always the same. There are those who regularly struggle with hurt, depression and anxiety and they need safe places to share their stories with people who understand and care. There are leaders who have learned to walk in joy, peace, and wisdom and they have much to share. The great thing about our twenty-four hour gatherings is that these leaders come together to help and support one another. It is a powerful dynamic.

The spiritual dynamic is vitally important. The twenty-four hour gathering is not just a fellowship and support time. It is a time for spiritual grounding, direction and conviction. In a typical gathering, after the opening meal (usually lunch), one of the leaders will share an opening devotional. This devotional, we have learned, needs to be substantive and rooted in deep conviction. A minister or pastor may prepare for it for a month beforehand or it may come from his best preaching/leading insights over the last year. It is not just the spiritual facts of the Bible that are shared--it is the heart level impact of what has been experienced. It is not unusual for a man to break down and cry as he shares at this level. The devotional time, because it is substantive, can last for 30 to 45 minutes.

Another component of the spiritual dynamic is shared prayer times. In some of the twenty-four hour gatherings we come together after a fun event, just before we all head off to bed, to pray. Some of the times we pray and it is just a good prayer time; other times we pray and it is a transparent, Holy Spirit-inspired, soul-transforming prayer time! At these deeper levels it is not something that one can anticipate. It is just something that God produces within the hearts of those who come together.

The missional dynamic, from a church planting perspective, is the most important dynamic, but there is a balance to all three dynamics. If the twenty-four hour gatherings are just relational and spiritual, over time those who participate will not be energized and entropy will set in. Relationships and spiritual support in twenty-four hour gatherings, without clear mission projects leads to a lack of momentum and excitement. Dreaming and achieving – the missional dynamic – when combined with the other dynamics creates a powerful synergy.

The missional dynamic must focus upon planting churches. It is important to be clear about this focus. Several of the networks we interviewed, including Converge, have experimented with another focus. The typical second focus leaders turn to is the "renewal of declining churches." While renewal is an important ministry, we have learned from others and from our own experience that it is a detrimental diversion from church planting. The biggest reason is that renewal takes far more energy, time and focus for significantly reduced results than church planting.

It is very hard to change the DNA of declining churches. In some cases it may be best for the existing church to choose to close and be resurrected as a new church plant. In fact, we have a funny statement, originally attributed to Rick Warren that we repeat to each other in this regard: "It is much easier to have babies than to raise the dead!" It is simply a fact that turning the focus from church planting to something else is a mistake if your primary goal is to plant churches.

In the missional dynamic we start by dreaming. When a group of church leaders has come together to support and help each other--and church planters started joining their meetings--it is easy to dream about what can be accomplished. In healthy twenty-four hour gatherings there are teachings about church planting: the need for church plants, how church planting works and best of all, stories from church planters who have joined the network and describe what they are doing.

Sometimes the topic of church planting comes up late at night as leaders talk to each other as they share a cup of hot chocolate or as they sit by the fire. In healthy twenty-four hour gatherings the topic will often come up by the morning sessions. When leaders come together in this environment the ideas and visions of what can be accomplished are significant. It is amazing to see the church planting ideas and commitments that men who are in relationship with each other will generate in these gatherings.

A good meeting always ends by focusing on getting the job of church planting done. It may be that leaders commit to plant churches in new areas, or they commit to each other to find funds that were previously not thought to be available for new plants or it may be that they commit to help find young leaders who will be great church planters. The driving, transcendent Kingdom mission of reaching lost people and making disciples gives energy, direction and purpose to these gatherings that make them more powerful than outsiders can easily imagine.

In an attempt to explain the combined dynamics of Lead Team meetings, Tom Nebel uses a description of one of the most effective teams in U.S. history, the Lewis and Clark expedition. This team accomplished more in their exploring and claiming the Western Unite States than most of us can wrap our minds around. They traveled up the Missouri river and embarked on a Westward journey that covered thousands of miles, through hostile Indian tribal regions, over mountains and the harshest of winter conditions, with very few losses and wonderfully successful results.

Historian Stephen Ambrose describes how they shared their lives and mission together:

> Teamwork. This was a family that had come together and formed a team for the exploration of the continent of North America. And they couldn't have done it if they hadn't become a family. Every one of them could recognize a cough in the night and know who it was. They could hear a footstep in the night and know who it was. They knew who liked salt on their meat and who didn't. They knew who was the best shot in the expedition, who was the fastest runner, who was the man who could get a fire going on a rainy day. They knew (because they sat around the campfire) about each others' parents and loved ones, each others' hopes. And they had come to love each other to the point that they would sell their own lives, gladly, to save a comrade. They had developed a bond; they had become a band of brothers, and together they were able to accomplish feats that we just stand astonished at today when we look back at them.[173]

We cannot think of a better analogy for the best vision of what teams of church leaders can accomplish and experience in a church-planting network. Over time, through healthy network gatherings and forged relationships, especially through the regular practice of lead team gatherings, leaders can form a tight, relational, spiritual and missional bond.

The Structure of a 24-Hour Gathering

LEAD Team gatherings are brought together by network coaches. These men are church leaders themselves who have been trained by Stadia to lead the gathering. In what follows you might think of them as "head coaches" because each of the participants will be encouraged to also coach and help others during the gathering. Here are the keys to the structure:

- Get a good location
- Start with the most respected local pastor(s)
- Gather six to fourteen leaders

- Meet together every second month

The network coach will typically set a date for the gathering and secure a good location. The best location is typically a hotel or retreat center with nice but inexpensive rooms (each participant will have to pay his own expenses) and a central gathering area for eating, teaching, coaching, dreaming and committing. It is also important that the location for the gathering be close to venues or places where a "fun event" can be shared by everyone participating. We have seen twenty-four hour gatherings work well in local hotels, ranch houses, retreat centers and even large homes.

The best way to recruit leaders to the gathering, if it is a first gathering, is to start with the most widely respected leaders in the area of the local network. By this statement we mean respected leaders who support church planting. This is best done by meeting the leader face to face and explaining the dynamics of a twenty-four hour gathering. Once a church leader has caught the vision of what can be experienced and achieved, he is likely to commit himself to attend the gathering. Because the network coach has been wise in securing his commitment first – as a well respected leader in the region – then others will be more inclined to join with him and the Stadia network coach.

Typically six to twelve pastors or leaders will come to these gatherings. If there are fewer than six, people may question the value of what can be accomplished or the energy behind the desired outcome. When there are more than twelve leaders, it becomes difficult to create a relational and personal environment. It is difficult for everyone to speak and share and give their input. The best number, in our experience, is between six and ten.

Once leaders have experienced a successful meeting, it is fairly easy to get them to commit to come back regularly. There is a natural rhythm in the cycle of meetings. If a group meets every month, it usually seems like "too much." If a group only meets every three months, it seems like "too little." The best rhythm, both we and Converge have found, is every other month (averaging 5 meetings per year).

In some networks the gatherings follow this schedule, but they may choose not to meet for twenty-four hours each time. Sometimes they start with a twenty-four hour gathering and then move to half-day gatherings, utilizing the twenty-four hour format only once a year after they have developed momentum. Each local network must decide for itself.

The 24-Hour Gathering Schedule

The schedule of the gatherings is designed to build relational, spiritual and educational momentum which leads to dreaming (vision) and action (achievement). The following is a typical outline of the meeting:

12-1:00 p.m.	Arrival, meal together, personal catch-up
1-2:30 PM	Devotional, prayer
2:30-4:30	Learning, training, coaching
5:30	Dinner, recreation, personal intercession
8:00 a.m.	Breakfast
9:00-10:00	Achieving
10:15-11:30	Dreaming
11:30-noon	Prayer for ministry

12:00 to 1:00 PM Arrival, meal together, personal catch-up

The first part of the gathering focuses on developing the rapport and relationships among those who gather. In the first meeting it is essential to introduce every person to every other person. There is something inherently relational about sharing a meal together. People talk, make jokes and tell stories to each other. Once a regular gathering has been established people will look forward to seeing each other and getting caught up on each other's lives. Sometimes the coach will ask someone to tell the entire group about something important that has transpired in that person's life or ministry. This relational foundation is the glue which holds all the other elements of the LEAD Team meeting together.

1-2:30 PM   Devotional, prayer

We described this part of the gathering earlier. The devotional time is substantive, heart centered and meaningful. As you can see from the time allotted to this section, there is often planned interaction around the topic. People are encouraged to share their reflections and reactions. This is also a time for substantive prayer. It is not the kind of rushed prayer that so often characterizes the gatherings of too many church leaders. The prayer time is meditative, meaningful and thoughtful.

2:30-4:30   Learning, training, coaching

In this section of the gathering, the focus is on learning, content and practical ministry issues which the leaders in the group are handling. The learning is often focused on the dynamics of church planting. It is an opportunity for the head coach to teach church leaders, who often do not know much about the practical nuts and bolts of church planting, how it all works and why.

The training portion typically focuses on helping leaders to learn about "ministry coaching" and actually coaching each other. Converge's Gary Rohrmayer is developing a twenty-four month coach training curriculum for LEAD Team meetings so that, after twenty four months, leaders can receive a certificate in coaching.

A coach, as we previously discussed, is "someone who comes alongside and draws out."[174] A coach does not tell someone the answers. Instead he or she uses questions to help another person figure out the answers. Converge leaders describe it this way, "coaching is the hands-on process of helping someone to succeed" or "coaching is the art of helping someone to do what they *don't* want to do so they can accomplish what they *do* want to accomplish."

Triads are an important part of 24-hour gatherings. Triads are groups of three leaders who listen to each other and then coach each other through big issues--personal or ministry related. As they gather into groups of three, one person starts by serving as the coach, one is being coached and one is observing. The person who is being coached may choose any "real life" situation in which they may need coaching. Examples could include:

1. A struggle you are facing in marriage or family
2. A ministry difficulty
3. An idea for an upcoming event or opportunity
4. A skill you would like to gain or improve
5. A spiritual or theological issue

During a triad coaching period each person takes a turn in each of the roles (coach, being coached, observer). A person is coached for twenty minutes, then the coach and the coachee pray for two minutes, and then the observer shares his or her feedback. The process can be very emotionally uplifting and practically helpful. For many leaders it is a highlight of the gathering.

5:30 – 10:00 PM Dinner, recreation, personal intercession

This is the fun part of the twenty-four hour adventure. If things are too serious and too intense, the experience is not as rich. To ensure balance the team will often go out for a meal where laughter reigns and then move on to a fun event. The meal should be a good one, often at a nice restaurant. The fun event is important to get everyone out of their comfort zone and engaged with each other relationally. We have witnessed local networks experience such fun events as skeet-shooting, laser tag, go-cart racing and bowling. By the time everyone comes back to the hotel or resort, everyone has loosened up and experienced an emotional outlet. This generally means that when people come back to spend some time praying with each other before bedtime, there is a good mood and people naturally let their guards down with each other.

8:00- 9:00 AM Breakfast

The breakfast time is actually a little later in the morning than would be typical in an intense seminar format. The reason for this is to give people a little extra morning time to first get caught up on cell phone calls and emails. It also gives people permission to stay up a little later the night before. Leaders will generally congregate together with one another and enjoy good conversations based on discussions from the day before.

9:00-10:00 Dreaming

Local networks need to dream big. Dreaming creates vision and vision propels church planting. It is amazing to watch--especially when a close relational and spiritual connection has been sealed in the previous twenty hours--how church leaders can create amazing vision. As they co-create, the synergy and attachment to the vision they create is amazing. Everyone is encouraged to speak into the plans. The group ends up owning visions and plans.

This is the power of local networks – everyone gets to buy into the mission, vision and plans. At this point in the gathering, the role of the network coach (head coach) is vitally important. He must make sure that the dream and vision is developed by the network and that it is consistent with the DNA of the network.

10:15-11:30 Achieving

It is one thing to have a vision and plan, but implementation is the biggest barrier that must be overcome. The process of actually agreeing upon an action plan is vitally important. It is also important to review the plans that have been previously made.

Again, the role of the network coach (head coach) is vitally important at this point. He must clarify the plans that have been made, the implementation steps that have been agreed upon and persons responsible. He must also make sure that the date and place of the next meeting has been established. Everyone is reminded of the commitments that they have made.

11:30-12:00 Noon Prayer for ministry

Since the dreams, vision and plans for church planting that have been created were brought forth after the previous day's prayers, they should now be sealed with prayer. The concluding prayer time is also a focus time for reviewing and praying about all the personal and family issues, along with their ministry issues, that have been brought to the surface from each of the leaders in the twenty-four hour period. A song or inspiring final word of prayer ends the gathering. The network coach releases everyone until the next meeting.

Summary

The 24-hour LEAD Team Meeting is a great tool which brings leaders together in a relational, spiritual and missional matrix that literally transforms lives and communities. This format requires a trained network coach who can bring people together and lead them into a successful gathering. The network coach also ensures that everything gets done that needs to get done between meetings. Without such person networks face entropy – everyone's responsibility is no one's responsibility. The coach is a highly effective catalyst for church planting in this environment.

Church leaders like this format because relationships with other leaders in ministry are formed and over time relationships can also be deepened, and strengthened. It is hard for busy church leaders, especially senior ministers/pastors, to form relationships with their colleagues in other churches but most desire to do more of it. Through the lead team meeting there is a regular opportunity (every two months) to make and build these relationships in the context of the all-important mission of planting churches.

The beauty of networks is that the members own the church planting-visions and projects they create. People own what they help create. Network leaders are invested creatively, strategically and collectively in the mission of reaching lost men and women through their plants. Church leaders don't complain about the planting projects to evangelistic associations or denominational leaders because they came up with the plans themselves

Once they are hired, church planters are welcomed into a support network with enthusiasm. Because they are an integral part of the local network from the beginning, church planters receive help and coaching from a team of leaders (especially when all LEAD team members are receiving regular training in coaching). This kind of support means the risks are reduced, the stress is reduced, and the success and effectiveness of church plants are greatly enhanced. By using the LEAD Team gathering we're doing together what we couldn't do alone.

And so we end with a restatement of our thesis: we are best off doing things together because it honors God and makes the biggest difference possible in terms of supporting one another in the work of planting churches … ***Together: Networks and Church Planting*** is what it is all about.

APPENDICES

APPENDIX I

Stadia: New Church Strategies
Network Coach Job Description
Compensation Agreement for Church Planting Network Coach

This contract is between Stadia: New Church Strategies and
_____, an independent contractor.

Beginning on _____, the coach agrees to provide services for 1-3 Church Planting Networks as specified below. Stadia will compensate at $_____, payable within ten days after the receipt of the written monthly coach's report to the Director of Mobilization. This contract will be for 9-12 months, depending on the progress of the MOUs as explained below.

Description of Services:

To develop a Church Planting Network that will plant a church and look to God to continue the collaboration by planting many more churches through the synergy power of church planting network(s). It is anticipated that this role will take 2-3 hours per week (10 hours per month).

Church Planting Network Coaches will:

1. Develop relationships with Independent Christian Churches/Churches of Christ in the area – or within the agreed upon parameters - in order to cast the vision and build a team which will develop a Church Planting Network.
2. Hold meetings with the Ministers/Pastors of the region – or within the parameters - to create passion and vision for church planting in the area.
3. Become a student in the craft of Church Planting through the Network.
4. Lead potential network participants through a process that results in a signed Memorandum of Understanding (M.O.U.) which describes the exact commitment each of the parties will make to

form a Network that plants a church, collaborates in ministry, and is mutually supportive.

5. Lead the Network to form a management team, and hire a church planter.
6. Lead in developing new sites and strategies for planting more and more churches.
7. Work closely with Stadia's Mobilization Team in developing up to 3 networks and being creative to make the Church Planting Network ever increasingly effective.
8. Meet monthly by phone with an assigned Director, interact regularly with other CPN coaches, and file a written monthly report that documents activity and outcomes of my work.

Reimbursement of Expenses: Stadia will reimburse the coach for auto travel at _____ and for snacks/meals incurred at face-to-face meetings related to the Network for up to $_____ per month when receipts are submitted.

Termination: This contract may be terminated in advance of the termination date by either party giving a 30-day notice in writing.

I accept this agreement and, in doing so, state that I am in accord with and will uphold Stadia values and beliefs. I also agree to abide by and to be supportive of the established policies of Stadia.

_____   _____
Coach   Date

_____   _____
Director of Mobilization   Date

APPENDIX II

MEMORANDUM OF UNDERSTANDING (MOU)
Insert location of church plant

This memorandum summarizes the understanding among the members of the *insert name* Church Planting Network (Network). The intent of the Network is to plant a new church in the *insert location of church plant* area with a planned hire date of *insert hire date* and a planned launch date of *insert launch date*.

The goal of the Network will be to recruit partners who will commit a total of $ *insert total* over a *insert number of months* month period. The following schedule lists each partner, the total amount of their financial commitment (cash and/or services) and a payment schedule.

Name of Partner Schedule	**Total Commitment**	**Payment**
Stadia: New Church Strategies	$50,000	$___ in services (see below) and $___ in funding

Note: Support checks are to be made out to Stadia and be sent to Stadia, PO Box 19700, Irvine, CA 92623-9700 with the following identification on the memo line of the check *insert State, location, and project code*.

Funds will be held in an interest bearing savings account with the Church Development Fund, Inc., until needed by the church plant. Stadia will manage the savings account and initiate withdrawals as directed by the Chairman of the Management Team and the Executive Director of Stadia.

Stadia is providing a Network Coach, helping to recruit, cast vision, nurture, educate, and coach network partners. The Network, under the leadership of Stadia personnel, shall establish a Management Team (MT) to provide guidance and oversight for the church planter and the new church project.

The MT is composed of leaders from the Network partners and provides guidance and oversight until the church is able to establish a local leadership team, not sooner than the church's second anniversary. Each network partner who commits a minimum of $ _____ will be entitled to have one representative on the MT.

1. By a unanimous agreement, the MT will decide the location of the plant, lead planter, and a church planting strategy (e.g. attractional, missional, house church, Compassion By Design, etc.). By consensus, the MT will provide oversight for the other major plans of the plant, including the launch plan and the financial plan. Staff hires that are not reflected in the financial plan should be approved by the MT prior to the establishment of a local leadership team.
2. The church planter shall not be employed until $75,000 ($100,000 if Stadia services are counted) has been deposited into the funding account (or other amount specified in the Financial Plan). This stipulation is necessary to protect the Network, new church project, and the church planter's family.
3. The MT shall strive to ensure that the church planter and the new church uphold this MOU and the Church Planter Expectation Document.

The Network partners agree to the following minimum standards:
1. Professional assessment of church planting team members and spouses, if married, for three years from the hire date of the lead planter. This includes any team member that works 15 or more hours per week in a ministry role that involves leading others or has consistent platform presence in worship services. Exceptions would be those serving only in clerical roles. Stadia minimum standards for professional assessment available on request. MT chair is responsible to monitor this

requirement. Cost of team members' assessment should be in the new church budget.

2. Professional training of the church planter and spouse, if married.
3. Professional coaching by an experienced practitioner.
4. The new church will be a Christian Church and will agree to follow Restoration Movement principles (see Affirmation of Faith statement in the Expectations Document).
5. The new church will be overseen by a Management Team approved by the Network.
6. Tithing to church planting is a principle that demonstrates our commitment to the Great Commission and to the value of church planting in a very practical way. The new church and church planter will agree to donate 10% of its general offerings to church planting, beginning with the first public offering for at least 10 years. ___% shall be paid to Stadia and ____% will be held in the network CDF account for future church planting within the network.
7. One goal of the Network is to start healthy reproducing churches that are committed to church planting and multiplication.
8. The new church will follow a financial plan approved by the Management Team/Network and will provide detailed financial reports to members of the Management Team/Network.
9. The church planter will create and implement a strategic plan.

In addition to providing a Network Coach, Stadia will contribute the following services (already included in the total commitment on Page 1):

1. Assessment of the lead planter and spouse, including registration fees, travel, and lodging ($2,500).
2. Initial training (bootcamp), including program costs, travel, and lodging for the planter and his wife and additional post launch training ($3,500).
3. Accounting services provided by a Stadia approved service provider for a period of 18 months ($7,800).

4. Church plant coaching provided by a Stadia approved service provider for a period of 18 months ($7,200).
5. Project Management up through launch provided by Stadia ($15,000).
6. Compensation for the MT chairperson through the church's second anniversary ($3,500).
7. Stadia will work to help with various other services including: lead planter family care, ongoing training and events (e.g. the Exponential Conference and Reproducing Church Experience training event after launch), connection events with other Stadia planters, and access to Stadia staff.

Acknowledgements

ABC Christian Church commits that it will provide a total of $_____ which shall include $_____ prior to the date of planter hire and $_____ per year for three years, paid according to the following schedule:

_____.

_____
Signer Name, ABC Christian Church   Date

DEF Christian Church commits that it will provide a total of $_____ which shall include $_____ prior to the date of planter hire and $_____ per year for three years, paid according to the following schedule:

_____.

_____
Signer Name, DEF Christian Church   Date

GHI Christian Church commits that it will provide a total of $_____ which shall include $_____ prior to the date of planter hire and $_____ per year for three years, paid according to the following schedule:

_____.

Signer Name, Management Team Chair   Date

Signer name, Network Coach   Date

Signer Name, Church Planter   Date

Tom Jones, Executive Director, Stadia: New Church Strategies Date

APPENDIX III

CHURCH PLANTER EXPECTATION DOCUMENT

Insert location of church plant
Insert lead church planter
Month Day, Year

This document is designed to assure that the lines of communication are clear between a Church Planting Network (NETWORK), Stadia, and the lead planter regarding policies and procedures during the church planting process. This document will refer to the project Memorandum of Understanding (MOU) and becomes part of the formational documents for the project with the MOU.

What the Planter Can Expect from the NETWORK and Stadia

1. **Financial and material support**.
   The Network, through the management team (MT), coordinates the dispersal of the investments made by the financial partners into the church plant. These dispersals include start-up items (moving expenses, laptop computer, software, sound system, trailer, marketing and others as agreed upon in the project budget), and funds for ongoing operations. The project manager assigned by Stadia will work with you, the lead planter, to create the initial budget to be approved by the MT. Major departures from the budget must be approved by the MT in advance of spending.

I have read and understand the above commitments: _____
(initial)

2. **Training.**
   The Network, through the MT, provides recommended resources for several types of training. These include the required Church Planting Bootcamp, a post launch training event focused on reproducing, and other events and services by speakers, trainers, Stadia staff, and regular gatherings at conferences, conventions, or Stadia specific meetings.

   I have read and understand the above commitments: _____
   (initial)

3. **Planning.**
   The Network, through the MT, provides you the planter and your coach (see below) with assistance in the development of a strategic plan as well as accountability for working this plan and tracking progress through Converge, an online tool monitored by Stadia project managers and your MT Chair along with the coach and you, the lead planter.

   I have read and understand the above commitments: _____
   (initial)

4. **Planter care.**
   The Network, through the MT, provides for the care of your family through a) recruitment, b) assessment, c) coaching by an experienced practitioner for 18 months, d) support for your spouse, e) training at bootcamp and next level training, f) required staff assessment, g) peer encouragement among planters and spouses, h) access to all Stadia staff and services, and i) training events.

   I have read and understand the above commitments: _____
   (initial)

5. Accounting services.

Stadia requires and supplies a bookkeeping professional to handle all church accounts for 18 months after you are hired. This service provider coordinates payroll services with an outside vendor, provides donor services, manages payables, produces monthly reports and even weekly cash flow reports for you and your coach as needed. When offerings begin, weekly offerings are tracked through a database and year end giving reports are provided for local as well as outside contributors. All necessary federal, state, and local forms are filed and this service provider functions as church treasurer.

I have read and understand the above commitments: _____ (initial)

What the NETWORK and Stadia Can Expect from the Lead Planter

1. Cooperation and teamwork.

I will lead the new church I plant to affiliate with the movement known as "Christian Churches/Churches of Christ" or the "Restoration Movement." In any Bylaws and Articles of Incorporation adopted by the new church, Stadia, an I.R.S. recognized 501(c)(3) organization, will be named in the dissolution clause so that any remaining resources may be reinvested in starting Restoration Movement churches.

I will not lead this new church to merge with another group outside the Christian Churches/Churches of Christ or organizationally affiliate with any denomination.

I will regularly attend Stadia and/or Network sponsored events and cooperate with the coach and service providers recommended or assigned to me.

I have read and understand the above commitments: _____ (initial)

2. **Growth and accountability.**
   I will provide the MT and Stadia, weekly reports (and others as requested) to keep them aware of attendance, financial realities, needs, and prayer requests.

   I will become a student of the church planting craft and technology. I will be a life-long learner so as to insure the health and growth of the church. During the first 18 months, I will regularly interact with my coach.

   I will develop a personal intercession team, and maintain regular communication with the members of this team.

   I will comply with the MOU requirement for assessment of all key staff, full time and part time.

I have read and understand the above commitments: _____ (initial)

3. **Financial issues.**
   I understand that health insurance is mandatory and I will be held accountable by the MT to maintain appropriate coverage.

   I will abide by best accounting policies and will communicate those policies and procedures to those in my church plant who are appointed to handle funds. I understand that the Network/MT requires me to use professional bookkeeping services with an experienced vendor and is providing these services through Stadia for 18 months. At that time, I may elect to continue with the Network vendor or make other arrangements.

   Neither I nor my spouse, nor any member of my immediate family, will be an authorized signer on any financial account for the church.

   The new church I lead will tithe to church planting and missions in accordance with the MOU. As leader of the new church, I commit that 10% of all general offerings will be given or set aside for church planting per the MOU.

I understand that the new church will be on a financial plan that will be monitored monthly by the MT of the Network. The MT must approve of the financial plan.

I am responsible to raise (along with my team), $_____ over and above the Network provided funds. If I am unable to raise that amount, the new church will be responsible for the shortfall.

It is understood that after the Network provided funding period, the Network and Stadia may be in contact with the donors and ministry partners I recruit to develop a relationship with them and promote future church planting.

I have read and understand the above commitments: _____ (initial)

4. **Movement issues.**
In keeping with the values of the Stadia church planting movement, it will be our intention to be a reproducing church by helping to plant other churches or campuses.

I will develop and maintain regular contact with my coach and other church planters with regard to reproduction, as well as keep the MT and other supporters informed about the progress we make. We will uphold the value of "planting before building" to assure the DNA of our new church is also reproducing.

I will seek to extend my ministry beyond my local church. I will become a partner in the development of a church planting movement in my local region.

I have read and understand the above commitments: _____ (initial)

5. **Doctrinal issues.**
    The following will serve as the theological basis of our new church:

    - We believe in one God: Father, Son and Holy Spirit, as revealed in the Holy Bible and made known in Jesus Christ our Lord.
    - We believe that Jesus the divine Son became human, was born of a virgin, ministered in word and miracle, died for our sin, was raised bodily from the dead, ascended to God's right hand and is coming again for his people.
    - We believe that the Holy Spirit is presently ministering through the Christian Community, empowering lives of godliness and service.
    - We believe that the Holy Bible is God-breathed, true in all its teaching, and the final authority for all matters of faith and practice.
    - We believe that Jesus Christ established his Church on earth to carry out his saving mission among all people groups and formed the Church to be One Holy People.
    - We believe in God's saving grace that calls forth from all people: faith, repentance, confession, baptism, and new life and ministry through the Spirit.
    - And we commit ourselves to the teaching, practice and defense of these truths until the coming of our Lord Jesus Christ.

In keeping with the historic Restoration Movement church distinctives, our church will only allow into leadership persons who have expressed their faith by being immersed for baptism. In addition, if my new church chooses to develop a membership process, immersion will be required for membership. We will also celebrate open weekly participation of the Lord's Supper.

I have read and understand the above commitments: _____ (initial)

6. **Termination.**
    I understand that my relationship with the Network and management team may be terminated under, though not limited to, the following conditions:

    a. A moral or ethical failure that hinders my effectiveness or the operation of the new church.

b. A perpetual unteachable attitude and/or routine failure to live up to my commitments to the Network/MT as detailed in this document.

This process will be effected by a request by the chair and ¾ of the MT for termination; or, when the MT is no longer involved, a request of ¾ of the local leadership team (in consultation with the major sponsoring organizations) for termination. The MT shall make all final judgments in these matters.

I have read and understand the above commitments: _____ (initial)

7. **Dissolution.**
   Should I lead my church to dissolve its affiliation with the Network or Restoration Movement churches, I understand the Network has the right to request and receive full reimbursement for any funds and services dispensed during the formation of this church.

I have read and understand the above commitments: _____ (initial)

Signed_____ (Church Planter) Date: _____
Signed_____ (MT Chair)   Date: _____

NOTES

INTRODUCTION

[1] An "attractional church plant" is one that is launched with a large public gathering of people. Today there is a growing trend to start "Missional-Incarnational churches" or "Organic churches" which do not depend on large gatherings.

[2] Mac Lake, interview by authors, 8 February 2011, telephone conference call, audio recording.

[3] Albert-Laszlo Barabasi, *Linked* (New York: Penguin Group, 2003), 8.

[4] Tom Nebel, interview by the authors, January 2011, telephone conference call, audio recording.

[5] Converge Worldwide website. http://www.convergeworldwide.org/plant-churches/plant-church (accessed 21 February 2011).

[6] Neil Cole, interview by authors, 6 January 2011, telephone conference call, audio recording.

[7] Ibid.

[8] Scott Thomas, interview by authors, 7 January 2011, telephone conference call, audio recording.

[9] Acts 29 website. http://www.acts29network.org/about/vision/ (accessed 15 February 2011).

[10] ARC website. http://www.weplantlife.com/about/the-mission/ (accessed 21 February 2011).

[11] Billy Hornsby, interview by authors, 3 January 2011, telephone conference call, audio recording.

CHAPTER ONE

[12] For in-depth examination embracing the concerns for Christianity in the emerging generation, see Gabe Lyons, *The Next Christians: The Good News About the End of Christian America* (Doubleday, 2010).

[13] C. Peter Wagner, *Church Planting For a Greater Harvest* (Regal Books, 1990), 7.

[14] Charles S. Kelly, *How Did They Do It? The Story of Southern Baptist Evangelism* (New Orleans: Insight Press, 1993).

[15] Thom Rainer, Surprising Insights from the Unchurched and Proven Ways to Reach Them (Zondervan, 2001), p. 162.

[16] C. H. Spurgeon, "The Wailing of Risco," No. 349. A sermon delivered on Sabbath morning, 9 December 1860.

CHAPTER TWO

[17] Gregory Boyd, *The Myth of a Christian Nation* (Grand Rapids: Zondervan, 2007).

[18] David T. Olson, *The American Church in Crisis* (Grand Rapids: Zondervan, 2008), 28, and Josh McDowell, *The Last Christian Generation* (Holiday: Green Key Books, 2006).

[19] Reginald W. Bibby, *Beyond the Gods & Back: Religion's Demise and Rise and Why It Matters* (Project Canada Books, February 2011).

[20] Olson, 175.

[21] Ibid, 183.

[22] Ibid., 26

[23] Ibid, 28.

[24] Ibid.

[25] Ibid.

[26] Ibid., 35.

[27] Ibid., 147; see also, Win Arn, *The Pastor's Manual for Effective Ministry* (Monrovia: Church Growth, 1988), 16, cited by Stetzer, *Planting Missional Churches* (Nashville: Broadman & Holman Publishers, 2006), 13.

[28] Stetzer, *Planting*, 9.

[29] Win Arn, cited in Ed Stetzer, *Planting Missional Churches* (Nashville: Broadman & Holman Publishers, 2006), 13, which is cited in Aubrey Malphurs, *Planting Growing Churches for the Twenty-first Century: A Comprehensive Guide for New Churches and Those Desiring Renewal*, 3rd ed. (Grand Rapids: Baker Book House, 2004), 32.

[30] George Hunter, "The Rationale for Culturally Relevant Worship Service," *Journal of the American Society for Church Growth, Worship*

and Growth (7, 1996), 131, cited by Stetzer, *Planting Missional Churches* 13.

[31] Alan Hirsch, *The Forgotten Ways: Reactivating the Missional Church* (Grand Rapids: Brazos Press, 2007), 68-82; see also, www.theforgottenways.com.

[32] Liz Furlow, "Nashville Mobile Market: The New Fast Food," *The Vanderbilt Hustler* (7 February 2011), 1.

[33] Hirsch, *The Forgotten Ways, passim.*

[34] Stetzer, *Planting Missional Churches,* 8-9.

[35] Tim Keller and Redeemer Presbyterian Church, "Why Plant Churches," (Copyright 2002, used by permission), 4.

[36] Ibid.

[37] Stetzer, *Planting Missional Churches,* 7, 8.

[38] Ibid.

[39] Ibid.

[40] C. Peter Wagner, Church Planting for a Greater Harvest (Ventura: Regal Books, 1990), 11.

[41] BCM David website. http://bcmddavid.wordpress.com/2009/08/19/what-peter-wagner-failed-to-say/ (accessed 28 February 2011).

[42] Keller, 2.

[43] Ibid.

[44] Ibid.

CHAPTER THREE

[45] Scott Thomas, interview by authors, 7 January 2011, telephone conference call, audio recording.

[46] Bob Roberts, *Glocalization: How Followers of Jesus Engage the New Flat World* (Grand Rapids: Zondervan, 2007), 23.

[47] Godin, Tribes, 1.

[48] Cole, 94.

[49] Ibid., 99.

[50] Tom Nebel, interview by authors, 10 January 2011, telephone conference call, audio recording.

[51] Todd Wilson, interview by authors, 17 January 2011, telephone conference call, audio recording.

[52] Ibid.

[53] *Ori Brafman and Rod A. Beckstrom, The Starfish and the Spider: The Unstoppable Power of Leaderless Organizations (New York: Penguin Group, 2006),*142-3.

211

[54] Ibid., 34-35.

[55] Ibid.

[56] Dee Hock and VISA International, *One From Many: VISA and the Rise of the Chaordic Organization* (San Francisco: Publishers Group West, 2005), *passim.*

[57] Ibid., 13.

[58] John Arquilla and David Ronfeldt, *Networks and Netwars: The Future of Terror, Crime, and Militancy* (Santa Monica CA: Rand, 2001), 7-8. Also cited by Cole, 94-97, and Hirsch, 200-202.

[59] Neil Cole, *Church 3.0* (San Francisco: Jossey-Bass, 2010), 97.

[60] Brafman and Beckstrom, 179-186.

[61] Billy Hornsby, interview by authors, 21 August 2009, telephone conference call, audio recording.

[62] Ibid.

[63] Thomas, interview, 7 January 2011.

[64] Ibid.

[65] John Worcester, interview by authors, 7 February 2011, telephone conference call, audio recording.

[65] Win Arn, *The Pastor's Manual for Effective Ministry* (Monrovia: Church Growth, 1988).

[66] Nick Boring, interview by authors, 14 January 2011, telephone conference call, audio recording.

[67] Mac Lake, interview by authors, 8 February 2011, telephone conference call, audio recording.

[68] Dave Ferguson, interview by authors, 20 August 2009, telephone conference call, audio recording.

[69] Ibid.

[70] Tom Nebel and Gary Rohrmayer, interview by authors, 21 August 2009, telephone conference call, audio recording.

[71] Ibid.

CHAPTER FOUR

[72] Brafman and Beckstrom relay the story in *The Starfish and the Spider,* 31-34.

[73] Ibid., 31.

[74] Godin, 1.

[75] Ibid., 2.

[76] John C. Maxwell, *The 21 Irrefutable Laws of Leadership: Follow Them and People Will Follow You* (Thomas Nelson: Nashville, 2007), 11-22.

[77] We use the phrase *apostolic leader* to denote apostle in this book because that's the language being used to make an implicit distinction.

[78] Markus Barth, *Ephesian: Introduction, Translation, and Commentary on Chapters 1-3*, Anchor Bible, vol. 34 (Garden City: Doubleday & Company, 1960), 32-36.

[78] Hirsch, 151.

[79] Ibid.

[80] See http://www.theforgottenways.org/apest/ (accessed 15 January 2011). See also, his upcoming book with Tim Catchim on the role of apostolic leaders in the world today: Alan Hirsch and Tim Catchim (with Mike Breen), *The Permanent Revolution: Apostolic Imagination and Practice for the 21st Century Church* (San Francisco: Wiley, 2011) about the five-fold ministry described in Ephesians 4, focusing on the apostolic element of mDNA (missional DNA) as he briefly describes it in *The Forgotten Ways*.

[81] J. Robert Clinton, *Titus: Apostolic Leadership*, Clinton's Biblical Leadership Commentary Series (Altadena: Fuller Seminary Press, 2001), 44-47.

[82] *Exponential: How You and Your Friends Can Start a Missional Church Movement* (Grand Rapids: Zondervan, 2010), 187.

[83] Neil Cole, interview by authors, 20 August 2009, telephone conference call, audio recording.

[84] Cole, interview, 6 January 2011.

[85] Ibid.

[86] Thomas, interview, 7 January 2011.

[87] Ibid.

[88] Thom, interview, 20 August 2009, telephone conference call, audio recording.

[89] Boring, interview, 14 January 2011.

[90] Tom Nebel, interview by authors, 10 January 2011, telephone conference call, audio recording.

[91] Thomas, interview, 7 January 2011.

[92] Ibid.

[93] Neil Cole, interview by authors, 6 January 2011, telephone conference call, audio recording.

[94] Brafman and Beckstrom, 129-131.

[95] Ibid., 120-129.

[96] Ibid., 124.

[97] Nebel, interview, 10 January 2011.

[98] Brafman and Beckstrom, 125.

---

[99] Godin, 61.

CHAPTER FIVE

[100] Godin, 1.

[101] Brafman and Beckstrom, 206.

[102] John Worcester, interview by authors, 7 February 2011, telephone conference call, audio recording.

[103] NewThing Network website. http://newthingnetwork.squarespace.com/ (accessed 23 February 2011).

[104] Dave Ferguson, interview by authors, 13 January 2011, telephone conference call, audio recording.

[105] Ibid.

[106] Troy McMahon, interview by authors, 1 February 2011, telephone conference call, audio recording.

[107] Ibid.

[108] Ferguson, interview, 13 January 2011.

[109] Scott Thomas, interview by authors, 20 August 2009, telephone conference call, audio recording.

[110] Nebel, interview, 10 January 2011.

[111] Mac Lake, interview by authors, 8 February 2011, telephone conference call, audio recording.

[112] CMA website. http://www.cmaresources.org/about (accessed 17 February 2011).

[113] Ferguson, 190, 191.

[114] Hornsby, interview, 21 August 2009.

[115] Ibid.

[116] Vision360 website. http://vision360.org/contentpages.aspx?parentnavigationid =1336&viewcontentpageguid=e4755411-1a1e-495c-91a5-b441c08682dd (accessed 23 February 2011).

[117] Bob Roberts, *Glocalization: How Followers of Jesus Engage the New Flat World* (Grand Rapids: Zondervan, 2007), 14. In chapter one of his book, Roberts notes: "The word first appeared in the late 1980s in articles by Japanese economists in the *Harvard Business Review* ("Globalisation or Glocalisation?" *Journal of International Communication* 1 [1994]: 33-52)."

[118] Ibid., 20.

[119] Boring, interview, 14 January 2011.

[120] Worcester, interview, 7 February 2011.

[121] Ibid.

[122] The column called "Distinctive Ideology" is a word or phrase representing *our perception* of how they are unique among these nine church planting networks. It does not necessarily represent how the network would categorize itself in all contexts. They may not use that one word or phrase for the organization as a whole—it serves the specific purpose of this study only.

[123] Cara Parks, "Egyptian Revolution 2011: A Complete Guide To The Unrest" (28 January 2011), http://www.huffingtonpost.com/2011/01/28/whats-going-on-in-egypt_n_815734.html (accessed 23 February 2011).

[124] Dan Hind, "From Protest to Revolution," *Aljazeera (English),* 20 February 2011. http://english.aljazeera.net/indepth/opinion/2011/02/20112131580638716.html# (accessed 23 February 2011).

[125] CBSNews, "The Face of Egypt's Social Networking Revolution," *CBS Evening News,* 12 February 2011, http://www.cbsnews.com/stories/2011/02/12/eveningnews/main20031662.shtml (accessed 23 February 2011).

CHAPTER SIX

[126] George Panikulam, Koinœnia *in the New Testament: A Dynamic Expression of Christian Life* (Rome: Biblical Institute Press, 1979), 74-75.

[127] Thomas, interview, 20 August 2009.

[128] Gary Hamel, Yves L. Doz, and C.K. Pralahad, "Collaborate with Your Competitors—and Win," *Harvard Business Review* (Jan-Feb, 1989), 190-196.

[129] Pat Masek, email message to authors, Feb 25, 2011.

[130] Lake.

[131] Thomas, interview, 20 August 2009

[132] Hornsby, interview, 21 August 2009.

[133] Stetzer, 316.

[134] Nebel, interview, 10 January 2011.

[135] Ibid.

[136] Cole, interview, 6 January 2011.

[137] Boring.

[138] Add reference information

[139] Worcester.

[140] CMA website, http://www.cmaresources.org/greenhouse (accessed 26 February 2011).

[141] Cole, interview, 6 January 2011.

[142] CMA website.

[143] Lake.

[144] He explains the three observations here:
http://www.launchstrong.com/secondary-plant-model.html February 26,
2011.

[145] Lake.

[146] Ibid.

[147] Cole, *Church 3.0*, 152.

[148] Billy Hornsby, interview by authors, 21 August 2009, telephone
conference call, audio recording.

[149] Tom Nebel and Gary Rohrmayer, interview by authors, 21 August
2009, telephone conference call, audio recording. see also his book Parent
Church Landmines for a fully developed description of parent churches.

[150] Ibid.

[151] Robert Logan, *Coaching 101: Discover the Power of Coaching*
(St. Charles IL: ChurchSmart Resources, 2003).

[152] CoachNet website, "Church Planting,"
http://www.coachnet.org/en/churchplanting (accessed 25 February 2011).

[153] Book or PowerPoint.

[154] Hornsby, interview, 3 January 2011.

[155] Nebel, *Parent Church Landmines,* 25.

[156] Lake.

[157] See http://www.twitter.com.

[158] Thom Rainer, http://www.thomrainer.com/2009/06/ten-reasons-i-
use-twitter.php (accessed 28 February 2011).

[159] Ibid.

[160] Mark Driscoll and Jeff Vanderstelt, interview by Mike Andrews,
"Technology and Mission," 18 January 2011,
http://www.youtube.com/watch?v=Pm-
EM2ELkYA&feature=player_embedded (accessed 2 March 2011).

[161] Gospel Coach website, http://gospelcoach.com/ (accessed 26
February 2011).

[162] Ibid.

CHAPTER SEVEN

[163] Ed Stetzer, "Life in Those Old Bones," *Christianity Today,* 11
June 2010.

[164] In my (Bobby) opinion, the best book on Millennials, even though
it is eleven years old, continues to be *Millennials Rising: The Next Great
Generation,* by sociologists, Neil Howe and William Straus (New York:

Vintage Books, 2000).

[165]Robert Withnow, *After the Baby Boomers: How Twenty- and Thirty-Somethings Are Shaping the Future of American Religion* (Princeton University Press, 2010).

[166]Ibid., 120.

[167] Ed Stetzer, interview by authors and Chad Harrington, 16 February 2011, telephone conference call, audio recording.

CHAPTER EIGHT

[168] Terry Martell, interview by authors, 16 February 2011, telephone conference, audio recording. The story and all quotes that follow in this chapter are told by Terry Martell.

CHAPTER TEN

[169] MissionInsite website. http://maps.missioninsite.com/Maps.aspx (accessed 3 March 2011).

CHAPTER ELEVEN

[170] See Robert E. Logan, Sherilyn Carlton, and Tara Miller, *Coaching 101: Discover the Power of Coaching* (Churchsmart Resources, 2003).

[171] Thom Rainer and Eric Gieger, *Simple Church* (Zondervan, 2005).

CHAPTER THIRTEEN

[172] Church Planting Leaders Fellowship, Spring 2010 in Nashville.

[173] Historian Stephen Ambrose, as he appeared on the Ken Burns' documentary "*Lewis and Clark*".

[174] See Robert E. Logan, Sherilyn Carlton, and Tara Miller, *Coaching 101: Discover the Power of Coaching* (Churchsmart Resources, 2003).

Marcus Bigelow and Bobby Harrington

LaVergne, TN USA
12 April 2011
223854LV00002B/2/P